WALKS ALONG THE THAMES

Leigh Hatts

GW00696705

Patrick Stephens Limited, part of Thorsons, a division of the Collins Publishing Group, has published authoritative, quality books for enthusiasts for more than twenty years. During that time the company has established a reputation as one of the world's leading publishers of books on aviation, maritime, military, model-making, motor cycling, motoring, motor racing, railway and railway modelling subjects. Readers or authors with suggestions for books they would like to see published are invited to write to: The Editorial Director, Patrick Stephens Limited, Thorsons Publishing Group, Wellingborough, Northants, NN8 2RQ.

WALKS ALONG THE THAMES PATH

Leigh Hatts

Patrick Stephens Limited

© Leigh Hatts 1990
Line drawings © Ken Hatts 1990
All photographs are by the author unless otherwise stated.

All rights reserved. No part of this publication may be reproduced, stored in a
retrieval system or transmitted, in any form or by any means, electronic,
mechanical, photocopying, recording or otherwise, without prior permission in
writing from Patrick Stephens Ltd.

First published in 1990

British Library Cataloguing in Publication Data

Hatts, Leigh
Walks along the Thames path.
1. England. Thames River region. Footpaths —
Visitors' guides
I. Title
914.22

ISBN 1-85260-207-4

Front cover pictures
Left: Clifton Hampden, near Oxford.
Right: The weir at Marlow, Bucks.
(*Photos: Richard Turpin Studio*)

*Patrick Stephens Limited is part of the Thorsons Publishing Group,
Wellingborough, Northamptonshire NN8 2RQ, England.*

Typeset by Harper Phototypesetters Limited, Northampton
Printed by Woolnough Bookbinding Limited, Irthlingborough, Northamptonshire

1 3 5 7 9 10 8 6 4 2

CONTENTS

INTRODUCTION

The idea of a Thames Path based on the towpath was first discussed over a century ago when river traffic had already started to fall due to competition from the railways. This century pressure mounted for a recreational path with optimistic reports from the Council for the Protection of Rural England in 1929 and the Thames Conservancy's River Thames Walk Committee in 1946. Later Hugh Dalton, Minister of Town and Country Planning, expressed hope that a long distance path could be achieved.

In 1977 The Ramblers' Association published a survey based on the work of local RA groups and three years later the Thames Water Authority gave 'general support in principle to the concept of a continuous Thames Walk'. The Countryside Commission's recommendations for a route from the Thames Barrier in London to the source in Gloucestershire were approved by the Secretary of State for the Environment in 1989.

This book samples some of the highlights of the Thames Path in advance of its opening as a continuous route in the mid 1990s. There is the infant and often dry Thames, the last remaining ford below Lechlade, a lonely medieval bridge and Docklands with both old wharves and new paths created by Europe's largest development site. But the book also looks ahead to the 21st century when the Thames Path is likely to start not at the Thames Barrier but at the estuary. Already there are calls from local authorities and RA groups for an extension on both banks to the estuary. Whilst two Essex shore walks have been included here, the most likely extension is on the Kent side where much of the path is already waymarked as the Saxon Shore Way. This book's final walk goes beyond the Saxon Shore to the Isle of Thanet which was once an important part of the estuary and depended on Thames shipping for its prosperity.

Walkers will find that the Thames is getting cleaner and more healthy despite the odd pollution scare — as at Wargrave in 1988 — and the 900 tons of rubbish still tossed into the river in London each year. In 1983 a salmon was caught off the Surrey bank for the first time in 150 years. Lobsters are again being caught off Southend and a seal recently came upstream as far as Putney where cormorants are now a regular sight.

References are often made in the text to Conservancy gates. These famous pale blue wooden gates were erected along the towpath by the Thames Conservancy which was absorbed into the Thames Water Authority in 1974. Where replacements are needed the new National Rivers Authority uses dark wood. Care should be taken to close any gate found closed when walking the towpath.

Reference is also made to left and right banks. Always face downstream to discover the left or right bank. Left in the case of the Thames means 'north' and right is 'south' so London's South Bank is on the right bank.

A few routes are not circular but in all cases the starting point can be reached by train.

Walk 1

THE SOURCE

—— 6½ miles ——

OS Landranger 163, Pathfinder 1133 and 1113

The little visited Thames Source in Gloucestershire is remarkably accessible. Kemble Station, where this walk begins, can be reached in just over an hour from Paddington. Countryside runs right up to the station and halfway round the route there is a historic pub on the old canal which for a time extended the Thames further west. Although the walker is likely to encounter some water, the source, as well as most of the canal, will almost certainly be dry. The walk starts at Kemble Station.

Leave the station by the 'up' platform and walk up the station approach road. At a junction turn left downhill to find a fieldgate on the right.

Looking downstream on the infant Thames from the Foss Way.

The Source marked by stones.

Kemble is a quiet village with an outstanding Brunel railway station which was once the junction for Cirencester. The local landmark is the church spire resting on a 13th-century tower.

Go through the iron gate — it has an unusual latch — and walk ahead on the slightly raised path over the field. There is a stream (often dry) on the left. After a second iron gate walk on below the old Kemble-Cirencester railway embankment (right) to find the infant Thames flowing left to right under a bridge. The river is fed by a spring below the nearby windpump upstream so there is usually water here.

The way is now left fording the (usually dry) tributary. Follow the Thames upstream and after about 200 yards bear half left away from the river to pass three isolated trees and walk close to a hedge (left). Go through the iron gate (with the windpump to the right) and continue walking on the high ground by the hedge. On coming almost level with a solitary house (over to the right on the site of a canal pumping house) begin to curve round to the right with the very shallow indentation of the Thames (which is usually dry by now). Head towards the right hand telegraph pole. Steps lead up to a stone stile at a road. The tiny tunnel for the Thames is in the bushes on the right.

Thames Head. The main road is the Roman Foss Way from nearby Cirencester to Bath. The large, usually dry, bed on the south side is Thames Head which in very wet weather is fed by water passing through the tunnel by the stile. Thames Head Bridge, 200 yards further east, carries the road over the old canal by Thames Head Wharf where barges from London once unloaded.

Cross the main Cirencester road to a gap almost opposite where an iron gate is set back. Go through the gate and look down on the Thames (right). Follow the

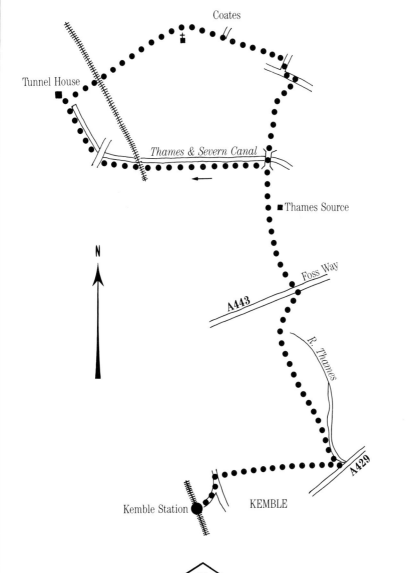

Thames Head Wharf buildings.

fence (left) to the far end of the field. The stone wall to the right of the gate is built to allow water to flow underneath when the Thames is in flood. Go through the gate and follow the line of trees (right) up the valley. Ahead can be seen the tower of Coates church (see below). Cross the wooden stile by the gate to see, half right under an ash tree, a stone marking the Thames source.

Thames Source is marked by a simple stone placed here in 1974 by the Conservators of the River Thames who were being absorbed into the Thames Water Authority. Old Father Thames, now at Lechlade Lock (see page 21), had stood here from 1958. Although the source usually appears dry there is, of course, water not far below the surface. The steep bank behind is the former canal (see below).

To explore the canal, the walk continues ahead below the trees and bank (right). A stone wall curves away to the left near the isolated Tarltonfield Barn. Go through the iron gate ahead and follow the field boundary (right) to a second gate where walkers go over the wall by way of a wooden step. Still keep ahead to a third gate where the way becomes enclosed. The path rises to approach a bridge on the canal. Do not cross the bridge but turn sharp left to go down on to the towpath of the former Thames & Severn Canal.

Thames & Severn Canal was opened in 1789 to link the Thames navigation with the River Severn by joining the Stroudwater

Navigation. The idea had been considered early in the 17th century and even won the support of Charles II. The canal ran from Inglesham (see page 23) where navigation now again ends through sixteen locks to the Sapperton Tunnel (see below). At first it was an important coal route to London from the Midlands but the opening of more direct canals and the arrival of the railways reduced the traffic. Eventually the Great Western Railway bought the canal but soon passed it to a trust which fell back on Gloucestershire County Council support. The waterway was finally abandoned in 1933 but now the Stroudwater & Severn Canal Trust is engaged on a long restoration programme.

This is one of the more overgrown stretches of canal although the towpath — the continuation of the path from Putney — remains clear. Soon after passing under the Kemble-Gloucester railway line, the canal reaches a former stop gate and round house.

The abandoned Round House on the Thames & Severn Canal.

Coates Round House was built in 1789 as one of five for lengthmen and lock-keepers including the Round House at Inglesham (see page 23). Because a prospective tenant here faced opposition from his fiancée to the odd shaped home, the canal company abandoned building these distinctive tied cottages.

Soon the path is running high above the canal. Follow the towpath under the road bridge and along the side of a deep cut to the long Sapperton Tunnel. Here there is a canal restoration information board.

Sapperton Tunnel is over two miles long and took five years to build by men working day and night in candlelight. At the time — 1780s — it was the longest bore tunnel and 'leggers', who lay on their backs and used their legs on the tunnel walls, could take a barge through in four or five hours. The men often suffered from a complaint known as 'lighterman's bottom'. The last boat passed through in 1911 but this southern entrance was restored in 1978.

The towpath ends above the tunnel in front of the Tunnel House Inn.

Tunnel House Inn was built in local stone by the Earl of Bathurst of Cirencester Park for the workmen building the tunnel. Now the house serves good food in a homely atmosphere with Thames memorabilia on the walls and, in winter, real fires.

Above *The Tunnel House pub.*

Left *Dry bed of the Thames near the Source.*

Right *Occasionally during winter there is enough water in the canal near the tunnel to make it again navigable to small craft.*

From the pub turn to walk over the tunnel and at once go up a bank to cross a stile. Keep ahead up the sloping field to another stile leading to the railway. Walk down the ramp and, after listening for a train, cross the tracks and walk up to the stile on the far side. Directly ahead, but partly obscured by a tree, is the tower of Coates church.

Walk ahead over the field — the path is usually left unploughed — to a gap in the stone wall ahead. Continue in the same direction across the corner of the next field to then follow a stone wall (right). The stone buildings of Church Farm can be seen clustering round Coates church. The path bears right to open out and run past the north side of the church.

Coates comes from the family name 'de Cotes' recorded in 1201. Much of the present church is Norman including the main doorway and font. The tower is Tudor and on its west exterior has a sculptured giant swallowing a human. The church was restored in 1861 under Canon T.C. Gibbs who served here from 1846 to 1914. Next door Church Farm is said to have lost tunnels running to the church and Hailey Wood behind The Tunnel House. The main part of the village, which lies to the east, has recently been slightly enlarged by the building of new houses in the traditional Cotswold stone. But this remains a very quiet area and the main event is the Coates Gymkhana where Prince William and Prince Henry, who live at nearby Tetbury, made their showjumping debut.

Continue along the now concrete farm track to a road. Cross over and go through

Church farm at Coates.

Water flowing a mile from the source.

the kissing gate. Follow the hedge (right) and pass through two further kissing gates. Over to the left can be seen the trees of Cirencester Park. Ahead is a gate and path leading to Coates main street.

Turn right to pass Bathurst Row (right). At the T-junction go left (as for Kemble, Tetbury and Cirencester). After 300 yards, beyond the grand Beech Cottage entrance (left), there is a stone stile on the right before a wooden gate. From here there is a view over the end of the Thames valley.

Go over the stile and follow a stone wall (right) gently downhill. At the bottom of the field go over a second stile under a tree in the corner. At once turn left to follow the wall (left) which immediately bears right to continue downhill. Just beyond a long barn (left), the path crosses the canal bridge encountered on the outward walk. Cross the bridge to retrace the outward walk down to the source and back to the station. For part of the way Kemble church spire will be visible.

LECHLADE & INGLESHAM

————— 3 miles —————

OS Landranger 163, Pathfinder 1135

To some Inglesham is the highest point on the Thames because it is the end of navigation. This short and delightful circular walk looks at the last lock, the highest boatyard and final Conservancy gate. The route runs briefly up the River Colne to allow a view of the confluence of the Thames and former canal which once allowed navigation to continue further west (see page 12). The walk starts at Lechlade church. Carterton Coaches (0993 842374) runs a bus service daily except Sundays between Swindon and Lechlade.

Lechlade town centre.

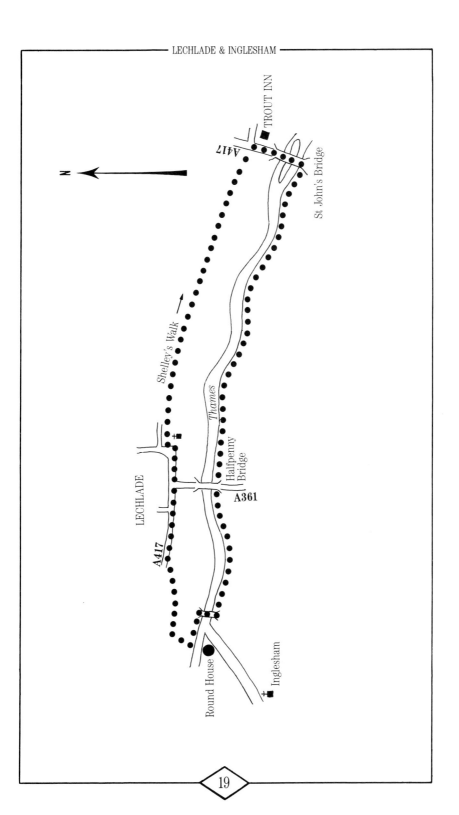

Lechlade. There was a settlement here as early as 2500 BC and the Romans came after building Cirencester. Thanks to the Thames, Lechlade remained a prosperous place even when they left and the small town featured in Domesday Book. The landmark church has been described as one of the six best in Gloucestershire. This perfect perpendicular building dates from 1476 and may have been dedicated to St Lawrence who came from Aragon at the wish of Catherine of Aragon who held the manor even after her divorce from Henry VIII. Her pomegranate symbol can be found on the vestry door. The rare Chapel of St Blaise, patron saint of woolcombers, has combs painted on the reredos and recalls the wool which was sent to London by river. Even before the Thames & Severn Canal was cut, Lechlade was a busy port for London. The beautiful very early 18th-century Church House in the churchyard was built by John Ainge who ran a wharf behind for landing London goods. The garden has a fine gazebo seen from Shelley Walk which recalls the poet's visit in 1815 when he stayed at the New Inn. He and his friends had rowed up from Windsor but found that the tolls on the canal would be too expensive to continue. Instead he stayed long enough to write *Stanzas in Lechlade Churchyard*. Later Compton Mackenzie featured the town in his novel *Guy and Pauline* and wrote 'the spire of the church remained so long in sight'. Although the railway closed in 1962 the town retains many of its services such as a library and the shops include The Flour Bag, one of the finest country bakeries in Britain.

Old Father Thames at St John's Lock.

The Trout Inn at St John's Bridge.

From the town square take the path at the side of the church known as Shelley's Walk. (There is a plaque on the left.) This is the beginning of a virtually straight ½ mile metalled path also known locally as Bridge Walk and Church Path. Beyond a lane the way is over fields with a glimpse of the river (right) and, after a second stile, Lechlade Manor can be seen in the distance (left). The path enters a long tunnel of small trees to reach a main road opposite The Trout public house. Turn right to cross St John's Bridge.

St John's Bridge. A series of wooden bridges here was replaced by a stone crossing in 1229 and soon after the Priory of St John was built on the left bank, the monks' duties including maintenance of the bridge. The remains now form part of The Trout, formerly St John the Baptist's Head, which has inherited the Priory's fishing rights. In 1475 Edward IV dissolved the priory, consisting of a prior, six priests and laymen, but left one priest in charge of the bridge. It soon fell into disrepair and Henry VII granted the bridge and its nearby chapel to the Dean of St Nicholas College at Wallingford (see page 57). About 150 years later General Fairfax rode over here from the south with troops ready to rout the Lechlade Royalists. After more rebuilding and court cases over ownership the present bridge was erected in 1886.

Just before the end of the bridge wall (right), turn right through the Conservancy gate and go down steps towards St John's Lock. This is the highest on the river and is graced by the figure of Old Father Thames who once sat at the source (see page 12).

The River Leach near its confluence with the Thames at St John's Bridge.

Continue ahead through the gate and on to the invisible towpath which runs across the grass and after a few yards leaves Oxfordshire (or Old Berkshire) to enter Wiltshire. The left bank is in Gloucestershire. Due to the winding river the way to Lechlade is not as short as it at first looks. On approaching Halfpenny Bridge there is a famous view of Lechlade church and the back of The New Inn where Shelley stayed.

The towpath opposite Lechlade.

Halfpenny Bridge. Apart from a nearby passenger ferry at the end of Bell Lane, traffic had to use St John's Bridge until Lechlade's own bridge was completed in 1793 following the opening of the canal. The bridge was made high to avoid the need to lower the masts of all the new barges which would be passing under. The arch stones are arranged radially as with the first Westminster Bridge which had just been built. The toll house remains inhabited although tolls ended in 1875. The ½d toll which gave the bridge its name was levied on pedestrians (except churchgoers and mourners) only until 1839.

Go through the squeeze stile and tunnel under the bridge to see the last boatyard on the Thames and, just beyond, Town Wharf at the end of Bell Lane on the far bank. Beyond the bridge the towpath is usually mown grass but this gives way to the usual worn track after a Conservancy gate. Beyond a sharp bend there is a good view ahead to Inglesham church standing almost alone. The path leads to Inglesham Footbridge.

Inglesham is the site of a lost village where only a 13th-century church and a farm remain. The church is now redundant but was saved from over-restoration in the last century by William Morris who loved its old simplicity and box pews. Although the towpath leads on to give a good view of the Round House it does not lead to the church. This is the end of navigation as the Thames, branching to the left, narrows and lacks dredging. The right hand branch marks the beginning of the former canal and the mouth of the River Colne.

A longboat approaches the limit of navigation at Inglesham.

Cross the footbridge to the left bank where there is a handy seat for watching craft turning on the river. Keep upstream with the path which turns up the River Colne for a very short distance. At a bridge the path turns right to join a track. Continue in a north-westerly direction on this track to cross a cattle grid and soon go through an iron gate to a T-junction. Turn right but when the track bears left keep ahead over a stile to follow a hedge (left).

Cross the first of four footbridges and bear half left across a field to another hedge. Keep forward to find the last two footbridges. Finally, follow a curving footpath to a hidden stile on the left. A short enclosed way leads to a low concrete barrier and the main road.

Go right to follow the road to the centre of Lechlade.

NEWBRIDGE & SHIFFORD

——— 9 miles ———

OS Landranger 164, Pathfinder 1115, 1116, 1135

Here the Thames' only remaining ford below Lechlade is crossed as well as one of the oldest and loveliest Thames bridges which stands alone except for a pub at each end. This is a lonely walk and plenty of time should be allowed for what on a map appears to be an easy ramble. But this is a circular walk only if the water is low at Duxford's ford which can be inspected soon after the start of the walk. Over-confidence is not advised if the river is running high. Indeed, locals suggest that the river runs extra fast below the ford. Plans can be made to walk as far as the Newbridge pubs. This makes a 6½-mile round walk and views are always different and rewarding when returning in the opposite direction. However, the river at the ford during a long dry summer can usually be paddled across.

Hinton Waldrist is served by Swindon & District bus 66 which runs between Swindon Bus Station and Oxford Station daily except Sundays (0793 22243).

Hinton Waldrist, a remote village on high ground above the river, still retains a shop and Post Office. The church is mainly 13th-century with turn-of-the-century glass by Heywood Sumner. The next door manor, a mixture of periods including 17th and 18th centuries, stands in a moat as the successor to a strategic castle.

The walk starts at Hinton Waldrist Church at the north of the village. (From the bus stop outside the Post Office walk up the lane to the west.)

Follow the lane which runs north past the church (left) and the entrance to Hinton Manor. Soon the way bends to give a view, even in summer when the trees are out, over the valley. Stay on the road downhill and at a sharp left turn go right to leave the road and follow a track past two thatched cottages (left). The way narrows and after 200 yards reaches a ford.

Duxford's ford during the summer — when it is often passable.

Duxford had a ford long before this reach ceased to be the navigation route in 1897 with the opening of the Shifford Cut (see page 33). The county boundary still followed this old course of the Thames thus placing the 'island' opposite in Oxfordshire rather than Berkshire until 1974. This crossing was sometimes known as Duxford 'Ferry' although there was no boat. A century ago the water was so shallow here that barges had virtually ceased to penetrate beyond Newbridge (see page 29). Between here and Newbridge there were other fords but only Duxford, being also an old towpath crossing, has survived.

Check the water level for the return walk which is made across the 'island' and ford. If rain has raised the river then the ground here is often wet, making the towpath a slippery shelf above the water. If conditions allow, stay on this bank to walk downstream on the narrow high path which is often some feet from the river. There are several Conservancy gates and at the second the way crosses a plank footbridge. The third tends to be overgrown and bypassed. On entering a field Shifford church can be seen ahead but on the far side of the river (see page 31).

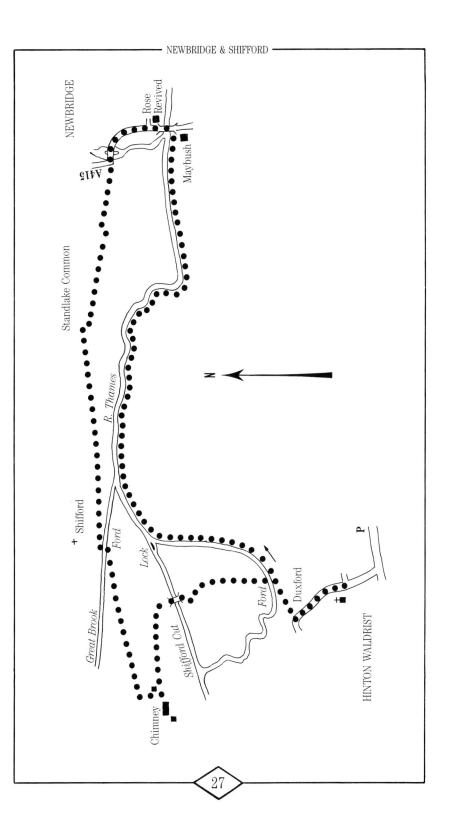

NEWBRIDGE

Rose Revived

Maybush

A415

Standlake Common

R. Thames

N

+ Shifford

Ford

Lock

Great Brook

Shifford Cut

Ford

Duxford

Chimney

HINTON WALDRIST

P

A view downstream from Shifford with the Towpath on the far bank where there is a Conservancy gate below the tree.

Soon the Old Thames joins the new navigation and there is a view of Shifford Lock at the cut entrance. The Thames Path proposals include a bridge at this point to reach the 'island'. This would replace the ferry which operated a few yards downstream after the towpath between here and Duxford became redundant in 1897.

On drawing level with the church it is possible to see the entrance to a creek known as Great Brook (see page 31). The path crosses an iron Conservancy footbridge (by a 'Beware of the bull' notice). Here, as a worn tread in the grass indicates, there is a tendency to cut the corner but since this is the towpath it should be remembered that the right of way follows the bank. The next iron footbridge, firmly marking the line of towpath, illustrates how much bank erosion can occur on the bend.

At another bend two railway sleepers carry the path across a ditch where there are newly pollarded trees. Pass through a double Conservancy gate before the river takes a large double bend north and south to where there are a few trees along the bank. After some distance the river bends south again to a wooden gate. It has been suggested that between the pollarded trees and here the river may once have had a less meandering course.

Stay by the river to cross a Conservancy footbridge over a stream which may be the remains of the old silted up course of the Thames. Now the way downstream is almost straight for the next 1½ miles to Newbridge but the path is again narrow (and sometimes slippery) as it runs through trees. At one point there is a Conservancy gate and stile side by side. Just before the riverside undergrowth and trees end the path rises to the top of the bank to follow the edge of a field.

Newbridge.

Pass through another Conservancy gate on to a grass path and ahead can be seen the stone arches of the medieval bridge at Newbridge. Cross a Conservancy stile and follow the bank as the pubs flanking the bridge come into view. The River Windrush is flowing unseen beyond the far bank to join the Thames at the left hand arch. Go through the gate on the inland side of The Maybush. Turn left to pass in front of the pub and cross the bridge.

Newbridge is 'new' because it is the oldest Thames bridge after the smaller Radcot Bridge upstream. Newbridge, with six pointed medieval arches, was built around 1250 by Benedictines from St Denis outside Paris who were then at nearby Northmoor. Afterwards they placed the bridge in the care of a hermit whose tollhouse on the south side has become The Maybush pub. The monks (whose work was only seriously restored in 1450) used Taynton Quarry stone, brought here by water on the River Windrush which joins here, and 400 years later Sir Christopher Wren had Taynton stone shipped from here to London for the new St Paul's Cathedral. In the 17th century this bridge was the scene of two Civil War skirmishes. The only other building here is The Rose Revived pub on the north side. Its inn sign showing roses being revived with Morland's ale is misleading as the name was changed back to The Rose after a period as The Crown. But it has also been called The Fair House due to the fairs held behind the building on the 31 March and 28 September in the 17th and 18th centuries. The pub, featured in *The Good Pub Guide*, is open all day in the summer.

Bank erosion on the towpath near Shifford.

At The Rose Revived keep on the right side of the road to walk 350 yards to a bend where the road crosses the River Windrush and its weirstream. Where the road turns north keep ahead on to a rough track.

When the track swings to the right after 300 yards continue ahead over grass and on to the narrow woodland path. There is often plenty of game here and after passing a house (right) the path bears right to a track. Turn left for a few yards to cross a wooden bridge into a field. Do not be tempted half left but go sharp right up the edge of the field towards a distant pylon.

At the corner of the field there may be a barbed wire fence to negotiate. Beyond the fence continue in the same direction. Over to the left there is view of Harrowdown Hill. On reaching a cross track go round the disused iron gate ahead to continue towards the pylon up the side of a field with a ditch to the right. Just before reaching the pylon, the way crosses a new wide track leading from the recently flooded Standlake Common pit (right). Beyond the pylon go through a double iron gate on to a track.

To the right the track leads to Standlake (½ mile away) where there are few buses but a taxi service operates locally (Standlake 236). (Walk through the village past the shops and turn left for the church and 'phone box.)

The walk continues to the left along the enclosed track to a wooden stile by a gate. Over a ¼ mile to the left are the pollarded trees by the river passed earlier. Keep ahead along the side (right) of the field. After just over ½ mile the field narrows. The Thames is now nearby but silent and unseen with its presence only sometimes betrayed in winter by swooping wildlife or in summer by the top of a passing cruiser.

Go through the iron farm gate ahead and across a small field to pass through

One of the green lanes on Standlake Common.

a second iron gate. To the right is Shifford Farm with the church a little beyond.

Shifford was once a large village where Alfred the Great held an important gathering in 890. The community's decline is probably due to economic reasons rather than a plague. The remaining church, once Georgian, was rebuilt in 1863. There was a flash lock here before Shifford Lock was built ½ mile upstream.

Now bear half left to pass under the overhead wires and, with a good view of the far towpath and the Great Brook, go through an iron barrier gate at the next fence. Continue forward with the Great Brook (left) to a pair of iron gates on the left leading to a ford. The church is over to the right. Pass through the gateway to walk through the water.

Great Brook was dug in the mid 19th century as an irrigation channel stretching back 2½ miles towards Bampton.

On the far side turn right along the edge of the field with the Great Brook on the right. But after just a few yards head for the left side of the pylon ahead. Go through a gap in the thick field boundary to go over a wooden stile.

Walk across the field towards the right side of the next pylon to find a wooden stile by an iron gate. Beyond here walk towards the end of the copse over to the left and climb over a wooden stile next to a double gateway. Now turn left up

Above *Great Brook ford at the lost village of Shifford.*

Below *Full flood at Duxford's ford in winter.*

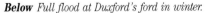

a road for ¼ mile to Chimney Farm. At the T-junction turn left through the Conservancy painted gates used by the Shifford lock-keeper.

Round a bend there is a second set of gates (the latch on the pedestrian one is usually very stiff). After a third gateway and a double bend the path divides before a high arch bridge. Go through the wooden Conservancy gates to walk over Shifford Cut.

Shifford Cut. Work on digging the cut began in 1896 and the following year the lock at the eastern end was opened. This scheme was not just to avoid the 1¼ mile loop and save ¾ mile but to remove a twisting navigation and open up the Thames again to barges which tended to turn back at Newbridge.

Once on the island pass through more Conservancy gates (usually open) to cross a wooden stile by an iron gate. Bear half right across the field to a wooden stile by a (probably broken) gate. Now go half left across a larger field to an isolated stile. Once over this stile keep ahead over two further fields and stiles. At the last field go ahead to find a stile in the centre of a line of poplars. Beyond, a short path leads past a wartime pillbox (right) to the ford at Duxford.

Having checked the depth and ferocity of the water on the outward journey: cross the ford.

Bear half right up a narrow footpath to pass two thatched cottages and reach the road. Turn left to follow the outward route to Hinton Waldrist.

Walk 4

OXFORD

———6 miles———

OS Landranger 164, Pathfinder 1116

The outward walk to Godstow, which passes the possible site of Oxford's 'ford', is a traditional university route taken on foot and water — Lewis Carroll chose the latter. Surprisingly the first mile is along a probably man made channel and the return walk via the Oxford Canal joins the Old Thames which made its way through the city as one would expect. Oxford Station, the starting point, was built outside the city which did not at first welcome the railway.

Oxford, founded on the Thames just before the Conquest, is now the university city with thirty-nine colleges — the first dates from 1249. It is also the home of Britain's oldest museum, the Ashmolean which opened in 1683, and Frank Cooper's marmalade first made by Mrs Cooper in 1874 and still sold at 84 High Street.

On leaving Oxford Station turn right and go right again under the railway. Ahead is the Old Gate House, erected in 1850 as the bridge toll-house and a pub since 1869.

Osney Bridge was maintained by Osney Abbey which stood to the south on the site of the cemetery at the end of Mill Street. The Augustinian abbey was founded in 1129 and by the time of the Dissolution in 1539 had such impressive buildings that Henry VIII briefly turned it into a cathedral. After four years that role was taken over by Christ Church and later Osney's stones were used as defences in the Civil War. The railway line from London runs through the east end Lady Chapel site. The main Thames channel at the west end was probably created by the monks to drive their mill. Osney is pronounced 'Oseney' and the present iron Osney Bridge, the lowest on the river, was built in 1888 after the 18th-century structure collapsed sending a child to her death.

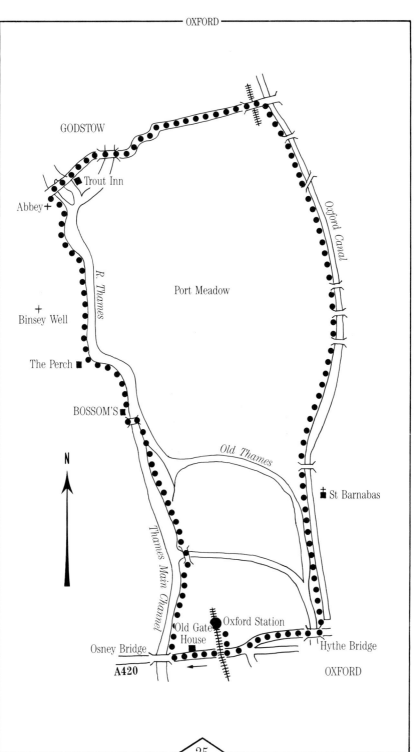

GODSTOW

Trout Inn

Abbey +

R. Thames

Port Meadow

Oxford Canal

+
Binsey Well

The Perch ■

BOSSOM'S ■

Old Thames

N

St Barnabas ✚

Thames Main Channel

Old Gate House

Oxford Station

Osney Bridge

Hythe Bridge

A420

OXFORD

Do not cross Osney Bridge but turn right on to the towpath. Here, where the river is believed to be man made, the channel is narrow. The towpath soon runs along the backs of gardens and over an arched bridge crossing a link to the Old Thames at a point known as Tumbling Bay — once a male-only bathing area.

Turn left to continue on the main towpath. For a time there is a stream on the right but where this swings away the towpath is on Fiddler's Island. After 400 yards the way passes between the new Thames (left) and the Old Thames. Do not cross the Bailey Bridge (right) leading to Port Meadow but continue ahead past Medley Boat Station which operates on the old river. Cross the arched footbridge from where one can look down on the river dividing into the two courses. On the right bank continue upstream to pass Bossom's Boatyard.

Left *Osney Bridge, the lowest on the Thames, at Oxford.*

Below left *The former Osney Bridge toll-house at Oxford.*

Right *The remains of Osney Abbey in an Oxford boatyard.*

Bossom's Boatyard. The Bossom family served as lock-keepers, weir-keepers and ferrymen for generations. In 1878 William Morris was towed by Charlie Bossom from here to Newbridge (see page 29). His grandson was the last involved in the business as recently as the 1960s. This spot was also known for the Medley flash lock — the last on the Thames — which was just below the bridge until 1937.

At first the towpath beyond Bossom's is a wide track which suddenly strikes away from the river towards Binsey. This is the approximate point of the ford which may have given its name to Oxford.

Ford. Until earlier this century there was a ford here which would have been used by pilgrims visiting St Margaret's Well at Binsey. St

Bossom's Boatyard near Oxford.

Frideswide's blindness was cured at the treacle well which later featured in *Alice's Adventures In Wonderland*.

The ford crossed to Port Meadow on the far bank.

Port Meadow, the vast 342-acre grassland, was given to Oxford as a common by William the Conqueror. 200 freemen have grazing rights and once a year the Sheriff of Oxford takes part in a round-up of stray cattle which are impounded at Godstow. The meadow's southern end floods in winter and occasionally becomes a popular skating rink. Racing was held regularly from the 17th century until 1848. The ground has never been ploughed or built on.

There is no need to be tempted on to the Binsey road as the towpath leads to the back of its pub. Go through the iron gate and follow the river. There is usually an abundance of wildlife (and often fishermen) as the river bends west to pass The Perch where there is a landing stage. A stile leads to the back garden.

The Perch. The 17th-century thatched pub, which has log fires in winter, is said to be haunted by a sailor. Children are welcome and there is even a castellated helter-skelter for them in the garden.

Towpath near Binsey.

The walk continues past The Perch and through the Conservancy gate. The river bends to give a view of Godstow Lock with the ruined abbey beyond. Cross the gated bridge and the edge of the field. There are often cattle here which drink from the Thames. Walk through the lock enclosure and keep ahead past Godstow Abbey.

Godstow means 'God's Place'. The Abbey, now in ruins on the bank, was founded in 1133 following a vision and consecrated in the presence of King Stephen. From Binsey (see above) Lady Edith Launceline had seen a shaft of light touch the ground upstream at Godstow. For a time it was a place of unofficial pilgrimage when the body of Rosamund de Clifford, Henry II's mistress poisoned by Queen Eleanor, was buried here. After the King's death the Bishop of Lincoln had Rosamund's bones removed from the abbey church.

The convent buildings were largely destroyed by Cromwell's General Fairfax who left the outline of the Tudor domestic buildings and a chapel. However the abbey hospice on the far bank continues to offer hospitality as The Trout Inn. Its garden is well known for its peacocks and ducks and there is a direct view back to the 'dreaming spires' of Oxford. This is the popular turning point for those on foot or water. In 1862 Lewis Carroll rowed here with Alice Liddell and her sister for tea on the bank and to tell them the Alice tale for the first time. The lock cut was opened in 1788 along with the bridge over the new channel but the weir-stream bridge is the old bridge of 1718 and the successor to the abbey-built crossing. The main abbey buildings were not therefore intended to be quite so near to the river.

Climb the bank ahead to the gate and cross Godstow Bridges to continue past The Trout. Soon the road crosses a Thames-side stream and the top of Port

Godstow Abbey.

Peacocks feeding on the riverside terrace of The Trout at Godstow.

Meadow. The pound for stray animals (right) was recently built to end the need to use the abbey ruins. The road enters Wolvercote at a double bend. Keep forward to pass the Baptist church (right) and the green (left). On the far side behind The White Hart is Wolvercote Papermill which produced paper for the Oxford University Press using water power from the early 17th century.

During the next few hundred yards move to the left side of the road which rises to cross the railway and the canal. Once over the railway leave the road and follow a steep path (left) down to Wolvercote Lock on the Oxford Canal.

> **Oxford Canal** opened in 1790 to provide a water route from London to the Midlands. This became the main supply route for coal until the railways proved cheaper.

Turn south to walk under the bridge. There is a glimpse (left) of Wolvercote church and The Plough which can be reached at the next bridge. The path surface varies and can be muddy in places. Soon there is St Edward's School playing field across the narrow water and the first of several drawbridges. From this point there are also usually the first of many houseboats. Another feature of this route are the numerous views of private waterside gardens on the far bank.

Soon after Bridge 242 and Lucy's Ironworks (left), the Old Thames flows in from the right. The towpath continues with the canal on one side and the

Thames on the other. After a short distance the path is level with a boatyard below the Byzantine tower of St Barnabas, Jericho.

> **St Barnabas**, inspired by the church at Torcello in Venice, was designed by Sir Arthur Blomfield in the 1860s. The striking Romanesque church, originally looking down on the Jericho coal wharves, was financed by devotees of the Pre-Raphaelite Brotherhood who supported the new Anglo-Catholic movement. This is 'St Silas' in Thomas Hardy's *Jude the Obscure*. Today the church remains a noted Catholic Anglican church.

Often moored here, appropriately, is a longboat which once brought coal on the Grand Union Canal from Coventry to the Ovaltine factory at Abbots Langley in Hertfordshire.

Where the path divides go over the left bridge above Isis Lock which connects with the parallel Old Thames. Continue along the towpath past the long line of houseboats — some with windpower and plants. To the left is Worcester

Boatyard by St Barnabas at Jericho on the Oxford Canal.

College and in winter the tower of Nuffield College can be seen ahead through the trees. This new college stands on the wharf where the canal terminated. Now the canal ends abruptly at Hythe Bridge whilst the Old Thames flows on to join the main channel above Folly Bridge.

Hythe Bridge. The first was built by Osney Abbey just after 1200 and the present iron bridge dates from 1821. Although the canal continued further this was known as Timber Wharf where not only wood but stone from the Cotswolds, hay and slate were unloaded.

Turn right over the bridge for Oxford Station (or left for the city centre). There is a map displayed by Hythe Bridge.

Walk 5

DORCHESTER-ON-THAMES

—— 5½ miles ——

OS Landranger 164, Pathfinder 1136

Dorchester once had a cathedral but that responsibility has long passed and even the through traffic now avoids the peaceful village noted for its abbey and St Birinus pilgrimage. This circular walk explores the towpath, the confluence of two rivers and a path high above Day's Lock but below the Wittenham Clumps landmark.

The walk starts at Dorchester Abbey. Dorchester is served by Beeline bus 5 which runs between Oxford and Reading daily except Sundays (0734 581358).

Dorchester-on-Thames was once known as Dorchester-on-Thame after the river which runs much closer to the village. This is an old Roman town with a 12th-century abbey containing the restored shrine of St Birinus who baptised King Cynegils of Wessex here in 635 and established a cathedral on the site. Winchester was later carved out of this enormous diocese, which after the Norman conquest moved its seat to Lincoln. The abbey church, which replaced the cathedral, survived the Reformation along with its rare 12th-century lead font, 14th-century wall painting and unique sculptured Jesse window to the left of the high altar. The abbey's brewhouse became The George Hotel, one of ten inns in the 18th century which served the main traffic between London and Oxford. The monastic tradition of hospitality is maintained in the original guest house which has become one of the best teashops in the country — open usually on Wednesdays, Thursdays and weekends from about 3.00 pm. The more tea you drink the cheaper it gets — 20p for the first cup but down to 10p for the third. The home-made jam is free 'while the day's ration lasts'. Well-behaved dogs are admitted but smokers are 'evicted immediately'.

Leave the Abbey by the south porch and keep ahead down the narrow path to a gate by the old toll-house (right). Bear left but just before the bridge turn on

Above *The George Hotel at Dorchester.*

Left *The 12th century font inside Dorchester Abbey.*

Above *Dorchester-on-Thames.*

Right *Dorchester's former toll-house in front of the abbey.*

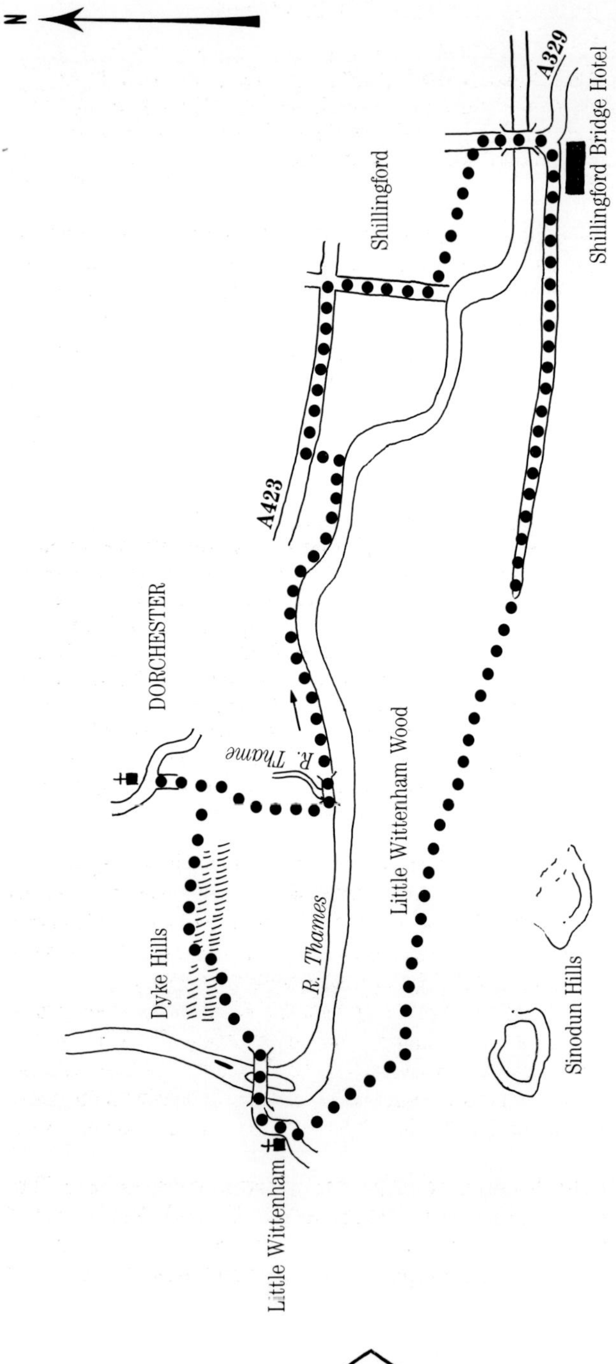

N

A329

Shillingford Bridge Hotel

Shillingford

A423

DORCHESTER

R. Thame

Little Wittenham Wood

Dyke Hills

R. Thames

Sinodun Hills

Little Wittenham

to a hidden path which runs down the outside wall to a low tunnel. Once through the passage go left to pass toilets and St Birinus Church.

St Birinus Church is Roman Catholic and was built in 1849 by a benefactor from nearby Overy. The architect was William Wilkinson Wardell, a follower of Pugin, who emigrated to Australia where he was responsible for Melbourne Cathedral.

Continue along on what is the former main road and just beyond the green (left) turn sharp right to go under a wooden barrier and up a short narrow hedged path. Turn left and where the track divides keep forward on to a footpath running down the side of a field.

Go over the wooden stile at the end to continue but glance right to see up the middle of the Iron Age defences known as Dyke Hills. The way runs through a narrow neck of field towards another stile. Continue to meet the River Thame at a bend just before it joins the Thames. Bear left over a gated bridge spanning the mouth of the Thame.

River Thame rises just north of Aylesbury in Buckinghamshire and its sheltered entrance is a popular mooring spot although it is impossible to travel up it even as far as Dorchester except in a canoe. It was in the Thame and not, as sometimes suggested, the Thames that St Birinus baptised the Wessex king. Some have insisted that the name Thames comes from an amalgamation of the names Thame and Isis (the Oxford name for the Thames). Others simply claim that from this confluence to beyond Oxford we should refer to the Isis rather than the Thames. The eroded bank immediately downstream of the bridge is Dorchester's traditional bathing spot.

Keep ahead on the river bank which is the towpath. Only where the river runs near to the road (left) just beyond a wartime pill box, turn inland to a wooden stile by an iron gate. (Although the towpath appears to continue it ends shortly at the disused Keen Edge Ferry which ceased operation about 1950. The name may be a corruption of 'Cane Hedge', a reference to osier beds.)

Cross the road with care in order to turn right and follow the pavement which is only on the far side. After just under ½ mile cross back at The Kingfisher on the corner of the entrance to Shillingford village. Turn down the road with the pub on the left. This is a beautiful street of houses and gardens with fine views of Wittenham Clumps on the Sinodun Hills. At the far end the road meets the river at a bend.

Just before the last house on the left go left up a narrow walled footpath. Turn right and follow a long enclosed path to a kissing gate. Turn left along a metalled lane where there is a view of the Shillingford Bridge Hotel. At the main road turn right to cross Shillingford Bridge. Here it is important to face the oncoming traffic.

Wisteria Cottage at Shillingford.

Shillingford Bridge, one of the finest on the river, is exactly half-way between Reading and Oxford and Windsor and Lechlade. There was probably a short-lived wooden bridge here in the 14th century and then a long gap until the 1780s when another wooden structure was erected. The present much admired ballustraded stone crossing was built in 1827. Although tolls were abolished in 1874, the toll-keeper's cottage remained downstream on the left bank until 1937.

On the far side at once bear right in front of the hotel on to a metalled road leading through the hotel grounds above the river. At the far end continue up a rough track marked 'North Farm Only'.

Keep up this bridleway as it rises away from the river. (The towpath is below between Keen Edge Ferry and the hotel lawn.) After passing through a wood, the way runs near North Farm (right). Just beyond the farm buildings (left) a footpath runs north–south on the line of a Roman road. But the walk continues ahead to pass the remains of Lowerhill Farm (right). Here the track gives way to a narrow path which follows the line of a fence (right) towards Little Wittenham Wood.

Little Wittenham Wood is part of the Northmoor Trust's 250-acre nature reserve. The wood is partly coppiced to produce wood for fencing and deer can sometimes be seen. The ½-mile woodland bridleway is well known for being muddy in places.

Thatched boathouse at Shillingford Wharf.

The path enters the wood through an almost invisible gap. Ignore all turnings and at the far end cross the stile and bear half right across Church Meadow towards Little Wittenham church. To the left are fine views down on to Dorchester and Day's Lock. Go through the squeeze stile on to the lane but before passing the church look back to see the steep path leading up to Wittenham Clumps.

Little Wittenham church, which has a 15th-century tower and font but a Victorian nave, was at first a daughter church of Abingdon Abbey upstream.
Wittenham Clumps The Sinodun Hills' famous beeches, which are being replaced by new trees, are partly in an Iron Age fort. Paul Nash first drew the Clumps in 1912 and his later oil version, *Landscape of the Vernal Equinox*, now belongs to the Queen Mother who hangs it at Clarence House. There are spectacular views of Oxfordshire from the top of the hill.

Turn right to pass the church (left) and follow the lane round a double bend down to the Thames. The path first runs on to an island to pass the lock-keeper's cottage and then over the main channel. From this second bridge there is a good view of boats entering and leaving Day's Lock.

Day's Lock only acquired the name in the 1820s having previously been known as the Dorchester or Little Wittenham Lock. Until 1875 there was a flash lock here. Now this is the main gauging station for measuring the flow of water in the Upper Thames.

Pooh sticks for sale at Day's Lock.

Go through the gate and bear half left across the field towards Dorchester Abbey in the distance. Pass through a wooden gate and follow an enclosed footpath which soon crosses the line of Dyke Hills to run along the north side. At the end there is the stile crossed on the outward walk. Bear to the left to follow the footpath back into Dorchester.

GORING & WALLINGFORD

———— 14 miles ————

OS Landranger 174 and 175, Pathfinder 1155 and 1156

Between the facing villages of Goring and Streatley and upstream Wallingford there is a choice of paths for the Thames Path. Much of the left bank is followed by The Ridgeway path running from Overton Hill in Wiltshire to Ivinghoe Beacon in Buckinghamshire whilst the right bank has a continuous towpath except at Moulsford. Here both sides are explored to make a circular walk.

The walk starts at Goring & Streatley Station. This long walk can be started even further downstream by combining it with Walk 7.

Goring church is Norman although at some point it was rededicated to St Thomas à Becket, and was once part of a large convent — the corbels on the south wall supported the cloister roof. The bell inside dates from about 1290 but the rood screen was erected in 1912 from wood which is thought to have come from HMS *Thunderer* in Nelson's Trafalgar fleet. Oscar Wilde spent the summer of 1893 at Ferry Cottage and his subsequent play *An Ideal Husband* includes references to the area such as 'Viscount Goring' and 'Countess Basildon' (see pages 65 and 68). Ferry Cottage was later enlarged to become the home of Air Chief Marshal 'Bomber' Harris who died there in 1984. The mill by the bridge, mentioned in Domesday Book and now a pottery, was the subject of an unfinished painting by J.M.W. Turner.

Leave Goring & Streatley Station by the main entrance and turn left and left again over the railway bridge. Just before reaching the river go right up Thames Road which is waymarked 'Ridgeway'.

Soon there is a view of the river (left). At the far end do not bear right but continue up a narrow enclosed path by Nuns Acre. The gently rising path later runs between brick walls before there is a view down on to the river. At a road go left downhill to pass, after a bend, Cleeve Mill (left). The late 16th-century building is now holiday accommodation. At the road bend keep ahead up the

Goring Lock.

right hand drive waymarked for both The Ridgeway and The Swans Way. (The latter is a long distance bridleway from the Salcey Forest near Milton Keynes to Goring.) The enclosed path rises and soon there are good views through the trees down on to the river and Cleeve Lock.

The way briefly joins a metalled road by the entrance to Ye Old Leather Bottle, a pub which has succeeded the spring here used in Roman times. Where the hard surface gives way to gravel there is a fine view across a garden to the river before the path becomes enclosed for 200 yards.

Just beyond a lonely cottage (right) the path runs out of the trees and across an open field towards South Stoke. Here one should be able to walk two abreast as the official width is described as 'two mules wide' in ancient documents. At the village go ahead up the main street to pass The Perch & Pike pub and the church.

> **South Stoke church** is 13th-century and has a 15th-century tower. Inside there is a wall painting and, in the north chancel wall, a memorial to Dr Griffith Higgs who was chaplain to Charles I's sister, Queen Elizabeth of Bohemia.

Where the road divides do not go right with the Swan's Way but turn left round the timber-framed house. At a second junction bear left again to follow a lane down to the disused Moulsford Ferry. Opposite is the Beetle & Wedge pub (see page 58).

Go upstream through the Conservancy gate to follow the towpath which has crossed from the right bank with the ferry. Here the line of the path is hardly

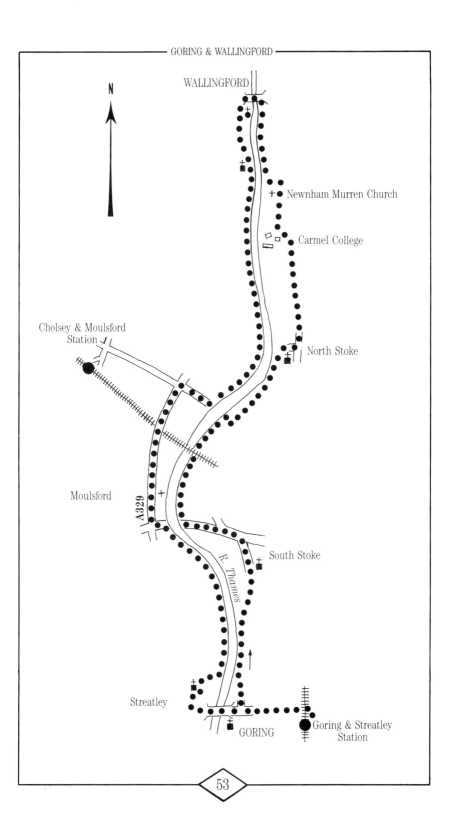

WALLINGFORD

N

Newnham Murren Church

Carmel College

Cholsey & Moulsford
Station

North Stoke

Moulsford

A329

South Stoke

R. Thames

Streatley

GORING

Goring & Streatley
Station

discernible as it runs over grass. Across the river is the back of Moulsford with its church's squat wooden tower and, at the far end, the back of Moulsford School. Pass through another gate before walking under Moulsford Railway Bridge.

Moulsford railway bridge was designed by Brunel and erected in 1838-9. In 1892 it was extended on the upstream side to accommodate two further tracks.

Go through the old gate on the far side of the bridge and keep to the grass bank. After two further Conservancy gates there is a view inland to Littlestoke Manor Farm and half left across the water to Fair Mile Hospital. Beyond a footbridge the way is briefly enclosed before reaching the former ferry crossing at Little Stoke which was once also a ford.

The towpath now crosses to the right bank so here one must turn inland for a few yards. Before reaching a cottage (left) turn left on to a signposted enclosed footpath running parallel to the river and leading to a stile. The slightly raised path beyond gives good views of the river.

On reaching a concrete footbridge go on to cross a small field by stiles. Keep northwards by the wire fence (left). Ahead in a line can be seen the houses of North Stoke. At a wooden stile, the path drops into a dip and becomes briefly enclosed and wooded before running across a large riverside garden. Suddenly the way turns a corner to give a view of a church tower before the path runs across North Stoke churchyard.

North Stoke church tower was built in 1725 but the church is medieval and has stone from the original Saxon building under the pulpit. Also inside are 14th-century wall paintings. The church is dedicated to St Mary of Bec following the marriage of a local Saxon lord's daughter to a Norman baron. Outside, over the south door, there is a possibly Norman sundial.

Leave the churchyard by the lychgate and walk down to the main street to turn left. After passing the mill (right) and crossing the millstream, the way becomes rough as it enters an avenue of trees. At the far end still keep ahead by the hedge (left) along the side of a large field. After a gap the path enters a second field which narrows on approaching Carmel College.

Carmel College is a Jewish school founded in 1948 and occupying the grounds of Mongewell Park which had a Georgian mansion until 1890. The estate was once a retreat for the Bishops of Durham and has a ruined church near the river.

Go over the wooden stile by the gate and keep ahead on a metalled college road to pass a lake (right) and a rare green telephone box. At a junction (where a signpost points to St John's Church) bear half right up a long straight paved path. After 350 yards The Ridgeway path turns right whilst the main path continues through a tunnel of trees to St Mary Newnham Murren church.

Newnham Murren church has a Victorian bellcote but a Norman north door and other very early work inside. The church has been made redundant as the village is now ½ mile to the north where it merges with Crowmarsh Clifford, which also has a Norman church.

Keep past the church but when the main track swings right go ahead over a stile in the corner by a house. Continue in the same direction along the side of the farm (left) and over a second stile into a field. Continue ahead and after a short distance (by a waymark) turn sharp left across the grass to the riverbank. The towpath has just crossed the river at the site of a former lock.

Walk upstream with a fine view of Wallingford with its famous church spire and bridge. On the way there are two footbridges with kissing gates. On reaching the bridge go through the gate underneath to climb up the steps on the far side and walk across to Wallingford.

Wallingford is on the old Wales-London road and 'Walling' is derived from the word 'Wales'. There was both a ford and a wooden

Wallingford Town Hall.

Above *St Peter's steeple from Wallingford Castle.*

Left *Wallingford Castle's modern drawbridge.*

The official Thames Path will pass through a Wallingford house.

bridge here when William I crossed on his way from Hastings to London in 1066. The present narrow bridge dates from the 13th century. The Normans built the castle which was reduced to ruins under Cromwell. The redundant St Peter's church with its candle snuffer steeple was designed by Sir Robert Taylor in 1777 although some suggest that jurist Sir William Blackstone, who is buried in the church, was responsible. The market place is dominated by the 1670 town hall which stands in front of St Mary's church. The Wallingford Bookshop in St Martin's Street is run by Mary Ingrams who is often assisted by her author husband Richard. The Harvest Bakery & Café in the market place is open weekdays.

From Wallingford Bridge, the walk continues ahead and left into Thames Street. (But to see the town centre keep forward past Thames Street and go left into St Mary's Street.)

Follow the road to St Leonard's church just beyond Riverside (left) which has a plaque to artist George Dunlop Leslie who lived here at the end of the last century. At the church turn left to follow a footpath past the east end, over a stream and under a house (where the 1894 flood level is recorded on the wall, left). On emerging from the tunnel turn left to follow a lane round to the right to join an enclosed footpath by the river. This is still not the official towpath, which is opposite. The enclosed path emerges on a concrete path by a boatyard. Here one can either take the higher metalled road by the houses or continue ahead through the boatyard. At the far end the way becomes enclosed and crosses a stream. The towpath opens out at the site of a former lock.

Wallingford Lock, known as Chalmore Hole, existed only from 1838 to 1883 when the ferry for the towpath crossing was re-established. The lock was only used at times of very low water and had tended to be left open. The characters in *Three Men in a Boat* were puzzled when they failed to come upon this lock shortly after passing Wallingford Bridge.

After a Conservancy gate the path soon crosses a substantial wooden bridge. There is a good view over to an isolated Victorian house inland. At a stile the towpath is level with Carmel College's boathouse and, half hidden in the trees, the ruined church (see page 54).

Beyond another stile the way becomes enclosed as far as a Conservancy gate. Across the river there is one of the many wartime pillboxes. Keep on past an eroded bank where cattle water, to a wooden stile. Here the path runs along the bottom of several gardens on a good grass surface before narrowing. At the end climb over a stile (being attacked by an eroding path). The way is now bordered by a wood as far as a bridge and a Conservancy gate. After ¼ mile there is a view of North Stoke church (see page 54) on the far bank.

After a kissing gate there is a view inland of Fair Mile Hospital (half right). Later, after a leftward curve of the river, the public footpath cuts the corner by running a little away from the bank on the well trodden line. Beyond barriers the path reaches Little Stoke Ferry. Here, as the towpath switches to the left bank and the way ahead is a fisherman's path only, follow the road known as Papist Way. The road climbs the hill to the side of Fair Mile Hospital.

At the main road only continue ahead for Cholsey & Moulsford Station. The walk continues left on the pavement along the main road. Just beyond The Waterloo pub, by the old Cholsey Station, there is a short gap in the pavement which is resumed at the railway bridge. Keep ahead along the road, which has good views of the valley, into Moulsford.

Moulsford. The little church by George Gibert Scott was built in 1846 on the site of a 12th-century church. Moulsford Preparatory School at the north end of the village opened in 1961. The riverside Beetle & Wedge pub is 17th-century and features in H.G. Wells' *The History of Mr Polly* and Jerome K. Jerome's *Three Men in a Boat.*

At the far end of the village turn left down Ferry Lane to The Beetle & Wedge at the disused ferry. Here the towpath can be taken up again. Go right and climb over the stile by the wooden gate. The resumed towpath passes moorings and reaches a Conservancy gate before running alongside a small wood to a stile. In the distance across the river can be seen the back of South Stoke's main street (see page 52). Now the way opens out with a view inland over to the Moulsford Downs and up Thurle Down Valley carrying The Ridgeway path.

At Rumford Hole by some pollarded trees there is a Conservancy gate. Beyond a stile the path is on the edge of a wide meadow. Cleeve Lock is in the distance and across the river is a view of the outward raised path and, further on, Ye Old Leather Bottle. Beyond Cleeve Lock follow the vehicle track but when the way begins to swing right rejoin the riverside at a Conservancy gate. The towpath runs under overhanging trees and, between a gap in the islands, Cleeve Mill comes into view. Soon the path runs over a steep lifting bridge and beyond a gate there is a view of the Goring Gap. After a further gate bear half right across the grass away from the river towards a Conservancy gate unusually far from the water. This is still the towpath, for barges used to be poled across the river whilst the horses were led through Streatley and over the bridge. This gate is at the end of a short wooden causeway. A tunnel of trees takes the way left and along another raised causeway to a lane which leads past the church to Streatley's main street.

Streatley means 'road' and refers to the Icknield Way which passes through here as The Ridgeway. The Romans created a ford which was succeeded by a ferry. In 1674 about sixty people died in a ferry disaster but the first bridge (called Streatley rather than Goring) was not built until 1838. The most famous building is The Swan on the riverside. In 1830 the inn-keeper was Moses Saunders who repaired weirs and started a boat-building business which eventually moved to Cowes, Isle of Wight and became Saunders-Roe. Impersonator Danny La Rue was a more recent owner of The Swan which is partly in Oxfordshire rather than Berkshire due to the mill being granted to the nuns of Goring in the 13th century. The mill, which stood on the

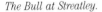

The Bull at Streatley.

Streatley's famous cheese shop.

opposite side of the road until a fire in 1926, features in the opening of Kenneth Grahame's *The Wind In The Willows* where Ratty's picnic takes place in front of a mill. The church was rebuilt in the 13th century by Bishop Poore of Salisbury who was responsible for his cathedral and its spire, but here the tower was not added for another 200 years. Streatley House in the main street dates from about 1765 and was for many years home of the Morrell family, relatives of the Bloomsbury Group's Lady Ottoline. Wells Stores at the crossroads, once run by three Wells sisters, is now the famous cheese shop belonging to Patrick Rance, author of *The Great British Cheese Book*. His wife is the daughter of Jan Struther who wrote '*Lord of all Hopefulness*' and other hymns here.

Turn left from the church entrance to cross the Thames to Goring and reach Goring & Streatley Station.

PANGBOURNE & GORING

————4½ miles————

OS Landranger 174 and 175, Pathfinder 1155, 1171 and 1172

One of the river's last toll-bridges and a high cliff are among the surprises on this short walk which samples the only climb on the proposed Thames Walk. This walk can be combined with Walk 6 to make an 18-mile walk.

The walk starts at Pangbourne Station but a return should be booked to Goring & Streatley Station.

> **Pangbourne** takes its name from the River Pang which joins the Thames here. The village sign incorporates a copy of *The Wind In The Willows* by Kenneth Grahame who lived at Church Cottage, with its prominent round toolshed, from 1924 until his death in 1932. His funeral was held in the next door church although he was buried in Oxford. Ducks Ditty coffee shop and wine bar in Reading Road has a *Wind In The Willows* theme. The riverside Swan Hotel features in Jerome K. Jerome's *Three Men In A Boat*. The nearby 17th-century Weirpool house, opposite the weir, was owned by actress Ellen Terry.

The walk begins at Whitchurch Bridge which can be reached by way of a footpath from the railway bridge by Pangbourne Station or through the town centre.

> **Whitchurch Bridge.** Although there was a ferry here this crossing could also be forded until the 1790s when the channel was dredged to accommodate the growing river traffic from the Thames & Severn Canal (see page 12). This is the third bridge on the site since 1793 and one of only two to maintain its tolls. Cars pay 4p but pedestrians, who were charged ½d until decimalization, can now cross freely.

Cross the bridge and pass through the toll gate to reach Whitchurch.

Pangbourne's village sign.

Whitchurch. The mill is mentioned in Domesday Book and the long main street, which includes two pubs, is lined with period houses. Recently the village lost its independence with the closure of its Post Office which sold virtually everything from food and wine to haberdashery and toys. The church, which dates from Norman times, is largely a Victorian building. In the north aisle there is a stained glass window showing Jesus at work with a saw in Joseph's workshop.

Right *Whitchurch toll-bridge.*

Below *Whitchurch Bridge tolls.*

WHITCHURCH BRIDGE

Tolls for Crossing this Bridge are normally collected each day from 7·30am to 7·30pm (9·0pm May to Sept. inclusive) but this does not affect the Company's legal right to collect Tolls at any time.

The Tolls for Crossing the Bridge each way are as follows:-

PEDESTRIANS & PEDAL CYCLES	Free
HORSES & CATTLE	½p each
CARTS, CARRIAGES Etc. (2 Wheels)	1p
(4 Wheels)	2p
MOTORCYCLES	2p
MOTOR VEHICLES (3 Wheels)	3p
(4 Wheels)	4p
(6 or more Wheels or fitted with Twin or Trac Wheels)	6p

There is a WEIGHT LIMIT of 10 Tons

By Order of the Committee of Management

Whitchurch Mill.

After the toll-bridge and before passing the Whitchurch-on-Thames sign, go left by the village slipway to enter the driveway to The Mill. To the left there is a view across the water to the bridge. Beyond the cottage (right) turn right up a walled footpath leading to the churchyard. Beyond the lychgate keep ahead on the path to return to the village street.

Turn left to pass The Greyhound. The street climbs the hill and just beyond the former Post Office (left) the pavement ends. Keep on past The White House and turn left where the sign points to Long Acre Farm.

The track runs ahead between a long wooden fence (left) and fields. Stay on the track past Long Acre Farm (right). After nearly ½ mile the way begins to run downhill and bear left to Hartslock Farm. Here leave the track by going through the small (and permanently open) white gate next to an iron gate.

A narrow steep path leads down into a valley and up the far side. From the enclosed path there is a glimpse back down to the river beyond a field (left). Ahead is Hartslock Wood (named after a lock which was at the islands seen shortly). On entering the wood (which is liable to be muddy) bear right on the

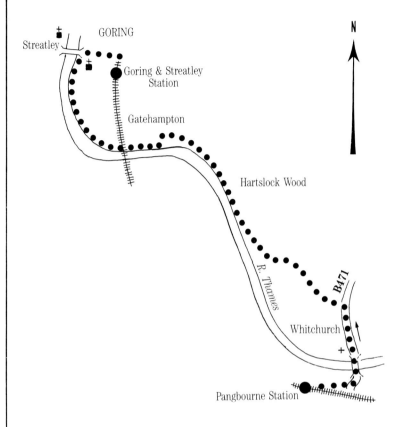

winding path which soon runs gently downhill. Soon the path runs along the edge of a chalk cliff with a sheer drop below. This affords the first good view of the river and the former lock.

The woodland path continues along a shelf on the hillside. As the path descends through the beech trees there are views of the river. A fallen tree trunk across the way has recently been cut through to maintain the path which also passes through arches of Old Man's Beard. The towpath can be seen across the water where there is the lonely Basildon church (13th-century with a tower of 1734 and agriculturalist Jethro Tull buried in the churchyard). This reach is often rich in birdlife from the Childe Beale Wildlife Trust to the east of the church and farm.

Where the ground levels out the path becomes enclosed and runs along the side of a field. Just before reaching Gatehampton Farm look out for a footpath on the left to walk down to the river. This path (which may not be signposted) leads to a backwater bridge and Ferry Cottage at the disused Gatehampton Ferry.

Goring Church.

Gatehampton Ferry Cottage marks the old ferry which brought the towpath over from Basildon. This peaceful spot has been under almost continuous occupation, as the recent discovery of Stone Age relics indicates. Near the railway has been found the earliest evidence of post-glacial man in Britain. In 1838–9 the building of the Brunel railway bridge and its embankments partly destroyed a Roman grain drier forming part of a group of farm buildings. The bridge was widened in 1892.

Turn right through a new TWA gate, a successor to the Conservancy gates, to follow the towpath to another gate and an open field. Go under the railway bridge and after some distance cross a wooden stile. Beyond this point many walkers have tended to create a new track by cutting the corner but the towpath continues by the river and at the next boundary one should cross the waterside stile rather than go through the gate.

Soon the way is in front of the first of several boathouses before becoming

Right *Goring Mill and Bridge.*

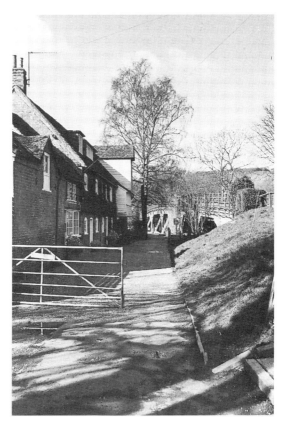

Below *High cliffs near Gatehampton.*

A beautiful thatched boathouse at Goring.

enclosed. This is a particularly delightful autumn walk when the chestnut trees begin to drop their leaves. After two further boathouses there is a view of Streatley Bridge before the path crosses an inlet near a picnic area. This is the old ferry point — 'Bomber' Harris lived in the former Ferry Cottage, now Ferry House, up the lane (see page 51).

Keep on past the moorings and beyond another inlet (with a view of the church), then turn right up the side of the Bridge and cross Goring millstream.

Continue ahead for the Goring & Streatley Station.

Goring (see page 51).

Walk 8

SONNING

———— 7 miles ————

OS Landranger 175, Pathfinder 1172

Thanks to the railway both sides of the river can be explored on this circular walk which has Sonning as its halfway point. However there is no Sunday service on the Henley branch line in the winter.

The walk starts at Shiplake Station which closes on winter Sundays. A return should be booked to Shiplake which is one station on from Wargrave where the walk ends.

Leave Shiplake Station at the north end of the platform. Do not cross the level crossing but go left. At The Baskerville Arms turn left into Mill Road. Soon there is a row of old cottages and a view (left) of Lashbrook Chapel next to Virginia Cottage.

At a postbox, by the entrance to the Red Cross Andrew Duncan House, turn left and before reaching the house go right over a wooden stile into a field. Keep ahead on the well used path to cross another stile and turn right along the field boundary. Keep forward over two further stiles to reach a road by the walled Mill House.

Mill House. Colonel Robert Phillimore, who worked with General Eisenhower on Operation Overlord, lived here as miller. Phillimore Island (see below) is named after his ancestor Sir Robert Phillimore.

Turn right for a few yards before going left down a metalled path leading to Shiplake Lock. But before the footbridge climb over the wooden stile (right) to follow the towpath. The tread across the grass here tends to be off the line of the towpath as can be seen from the position of the Conservancy gate and following stile. On coming level with Phillimore's Island, the path runs below Shiplake House. Beyond an inlet the way continues straight ahead with the river to below Shiplake College.

Riverside gateway at Sonning.

Shiplake College was founded in 1959 and the boys regularly row on the river making this a lively reach even on misty winter days. A footpath leads up to the church where in 1850 Tennyson married a relative of the vicar's wife. The 18th-century glass in the windows comes from France where it survived the Revolution by being buried.

Continue over an inlet by a boathouse into a field and soon the river divides at another island, The Lynch. At a bend the path briefly moves away from the water and beyond a small wood enters another field. Here the river is slightly screened by a line of trees and at another river bend the path is again away from the water.

As the path rejoins the riverbank there is a view across to the entrance to St Patrick's Stream. From here there is a dual path as far as Sonning. The towpath continues ahead with three more stiles to cross before reaching a wood on the edge of Sonning. There are two interesting old iron gates (right) belonging to The French Horn Hotel before the path crosses the river to the Sonning island. This is the home of The Mill at Sonning Theatre Restaurant. Turn left to go over the 18th-century bridge to the main village.

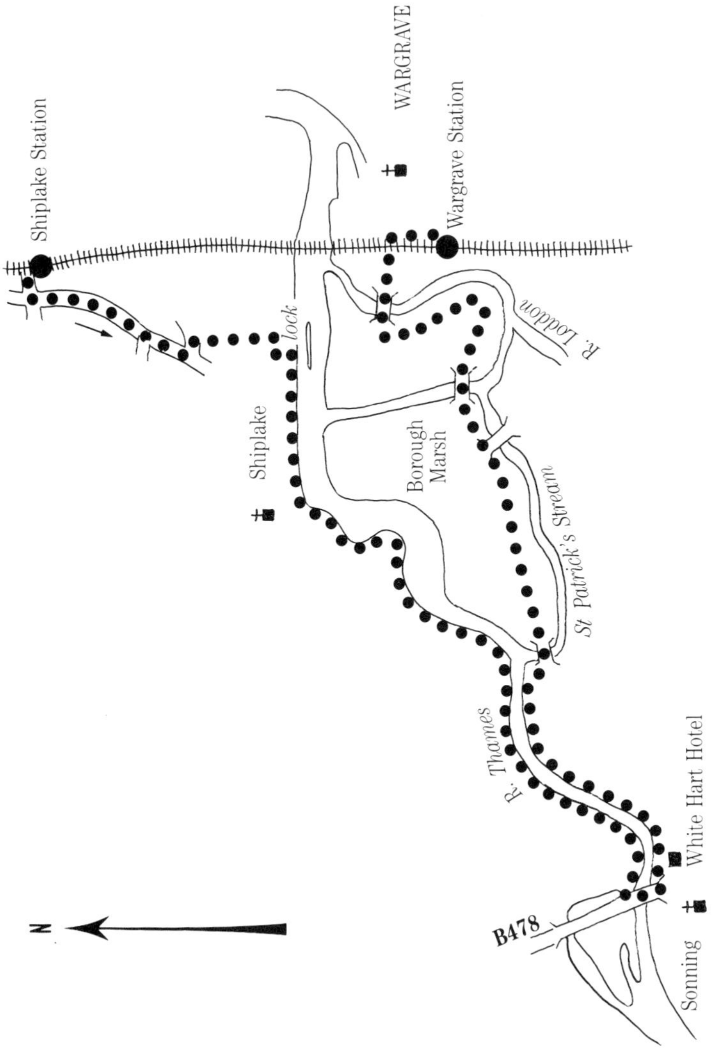

Shiplake Station

WARGRAVE

Wargrave Station

R. Loddon

lock

Shiplake

Borough
Marsh

St Patrick's Stream

R. Thames

White Hart Hotel

B478

Sonning

N

Sonning church.

Sonning is unusual in that it straddles both banks and is therefore in both Berkshire and Oxfordshire. Until Elizabeth I's reign the Bishops of Salisbury had a palace here next to the church. Now the most famous building is Deanery Gardens, designed by Edwin Lutyens in the 1890s with grounds incorporating the bishops' 16th-century walled garden laid out by Gertrude Jekyll. The White Hart, once popular with bargees, dates from 1200 and apart from its numerous food guide mentions is noted for Nickel, a forty-year-old parrot. There was a wooden bridge here, maintained by the bishop, in the 15th century and the present elegant structure dates from 1772.

The walk continues downstream in front of The White Hart. Go over the stile with the conical posts and soon the gravel gives way to mown grass. There is a view over the water to the towpath taken on the outward walk. However, since the right bank path is not a towpath it soon moves away from the water to run parallel but separated by a strip of trees and undergrowth for ½ mile. After just over a mile the path becomes enclosed and bears inland to join a driveway from a riverside house.

At a junction turn left to cross St Patrick's Bridge, spanning St Patrick's Stream, to go on to a large island known as Borough Marsh. The lane ahead serves several Thames-side dwellings including The Cottage with its thatched roof. At the far end go over a wooden stile and bear half right over a large field. In the north-east corner, by St Patrick's Stream, there is a wooden stile by an iron fieldgate. Go over the stile and follow a wide curving waterside path to a wooden

The entrance to the riverside path at Sonning.

stile by a track. Do not go over the bridge but turn left. The wide track narrows before crossing another stream.

A lane runs ahead past The Cottage (right) and soon enjoys a metalled surface. After ¼ mile the way bends left at Cherry Eyot (on the River Loddon). On reaching a crossroads turn right to go over a high bridge spanning the River

A thatched cottage at Borough Marsh.

Above *Sonning Bridge.*

Left *Wargrave church.*

The wide bend in the river at Wargrave.

Loddon which rises in Hampshire. The road continues ahead and after a bend has a concrete surface. Pass under the railway bridge and turn right to reach Wargrave Station.

Wargrave was 'Weregrave' when Edward the Confessor's wife held the manor. But there is no mention of a church until the early 12th century when it was served by Reading Abbey. This may have led to the use of the church in 1371 for the consecration of a new bishop of Lincoln. The tower of 1635 survived a mysterious fire in 1914 which destroyed most of the building. Arson by suffragettes or someone angry at the vicar's insistence at the word 'obey' in the marriage service have been suggested as the cause. The tomb in the churchyard claimed as Madame Tussaud's is in fact her daughter-in-law's. Lutyens designed both the Hannen Mausoleum in the south-east corner and the war memorial on The Mill Green.

HENLEY

——— 5 miles ———

OS Landranger 175, Pathfinder 1156

The Henley Royal Regatta, founded in 1839, is held in the first week in July. Out of season a walk up the 1-mile 450-yard Regatta course has much to recommend it in addition to the lack of crowds. The path is very easy going — metalled at first — and fine views continue in the valley round the river bend near Hambledon Lock. The very first Oxford & Cambridge Boat Race was rowed from Hambledon to Henley in 1829. The walk's halfway point is the excellent Flower Pot Inn and the overland return route offers a high view of the river.

The walk starts at Henley-on-Thames Station which is closed on Sundays.

Henley-on-Thames church, first recorded in 1204, was at first served by monks from Dorchester upstream (see page 43). The present building dates from about 1400 like the next door Chantry House. The church tower, added in 1550, contains a monument to William Hayward who designed Henley Bridge but died in 1782 before its construction. Horace Walpole was to describe it as 'the most beautiful in the world after the Ponti di Trinita at Florence'. In the 14th century the bridge had buildings including a chapel on it, like London Bridge. The Angel on the left bank is 14th-century and now looks across not at the 18th-century Carpenters Arms but the new Henley Royal Regatta headquarters designed by Terry Farrell who was responsible for TV-AM's 'egg cup' building. Just opposite the church is Speaker's House, birthplace of the Long Parliament's Speaker Lenthall. The next door Viceroy Tandoori has a plaque recording the visit of Queen Mary in 1931. The Red Lion has received Charles I. Henley is the setting for John Mortimer's *Paradise Postponed* which was filmed here for television

Turn right from Henley Station to reach the river. Cross Henley Bridge and at once turn left by a house called 'Tollgate' to find the enclosed start of the towpath which runs directly north with a metalled surface. This is the Henley Regatta

The new Henley Royal Regatta headquarters designed by Terry Farrell.

mile with the Temple Island folly in the distance.

Henley, seen nestling on the far bank, sometimes gives off a distinctive aroma created by its brewery. On the hill to the right is Remenham Wood visited on the return route. Almost immediately there is a rural setting on both banks. The

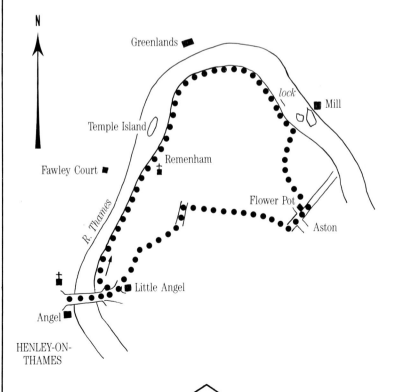

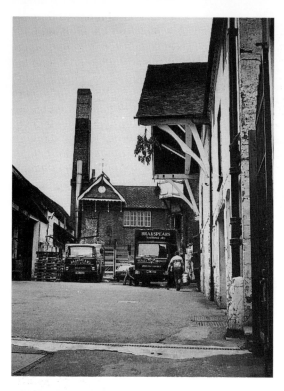

Left Brakspear's Brewery at Henley.

Right A Henley pub sign depicts the Royal Barge passing the Temple Island folly.

path passes through several Conservancy gates by a few attractive houses. Beyond the Remenham Club there is a view ahead to Remenham village and its church. But before Remenham is reached there is a view across the water to Fawley Court.

Fawley Court was designed by Sir Christopher Wren in 1684 but parts of a Norman manor remain. The grounds were landscaped by 'Capability' Brown. Visitors have included William of Orange and William IV. In 1953 the Marian Fathers opened a school there for the children of Polish exiles. Now known sometimes as 'Poland-on-Thames', the house contains many Polish treasures in its museum.

A few yards further on a stile on the right indicates the footpath to Remenham church.

Remenham is a tiny hamlet rather than a real village but its church has a huge parish — everything opposite Henley from Aston to the south of Henley Bridge. The church is mainly an 1870 restoration but the apse is on the line of the east end of its Norman predecessor and the tower dates from 1838. Caleb Gould, Hambledon Lock-keeper from 1777 to 1836, is buried in the churchyard. A ¼ mile further on is Temple Island.

Temple Island was bought for £½m in 1987 by the Henley Royal Regatta which feared commercialization if it fell into other hands. It had been owned by the same family since Fawley Court (see above) sold the island over 150 years ago. Its famous folly, used as a fishing lodge, was built in 1771 and designed by James Wyatt as the focal point of a vista from Fawley Court where he had undertaken some interior alterations. The folly was called the 'Devil's Temple' by Fawley Court's post-war schoolboys who used it for illicit smoking. The little building, which has frescos by Wyatt, has been restored recently and the island's trees thinned.

Beyond the island the river begins to bend eastwards and the towpath passes through a kissing gate. Above the river is an impressive range of hills topped with trees. Now the path is over grass with a good view of the white-painted Greenlands mansion across the water.

Greenlands dates from 1853 and was the home of W.H. Smith, the newsagent and bookseller and also Navy Minister under Queen

Temple Island at Henley.

Victoria who was parodied as *Ruler of the Queen's Navee* in Gilbert & Sullivan. The house is now occupied by the Henley Management Training College.

After nearly ½ mile the path reaches Hambledon Lock.

A canoeist at Hambledon Weir.

Cottage at Aston.

Hambledon Lock is a mile from Hambledon village which is up a valley to the north. The attractive mill building dates from the 16th century and was working until 1958. In George III's reign lock-keeper Caleb Gould (see above) sold home-made bread to passing barges. The long weir bridge, reached from the side of the lock-keeper's cottage, is a public footpath and makes an exciting walk across the rushing water. However, Mill End on the left bank is spoilt by relentless traffic which virtually precludes walking upstream to find the left bank footpath beyond Greenlands.

The walk does not cross the lock but stays on the right bank. Go through the wooden gate and larger iron gate to follow the rough lock road. Stay on the track as it turns inland towards some trees. The way winds up the hill towards The Flower Pot Inn which soon comes into view beyond a belt of trees. Where the path divides at a bend near the pub, keep ahead up a narrow footpath to Aston's Ferry Lane. Turn right for The Flower Pot.

The Flower Pot, according to old signs painted on the outside walls, welcomes 'fishing and boating parties'. This Edwardian pub has a friendly landlord serving local Henley beer and good food including substantial cheese sandwiches. One bar even has a shelf of books and there are old Thames prints on the walls.

From the pub continue inland up the road and (unless joining Walk 10) continue past the left turning to pass between Wysteria and Highway Cottages. Then turn right to follow the brick wall of Highway Cottage's garden. The path runs uphill under the fruit trees to a stile. Keep ahead over grass to join a track at a bend.

Go forward on to the track which (in winter) has views through the trees to the Thames. After the way runs downhill there are magnificent views across the riverbend and up the wooded valleys behind. Hambledon can be seen above Mill End and gleaming Greenlands below the next valley. Just beyond a copse (left) the track meets a road.

Turn left to a gap in the right-hand hedge just below the lonely oak tree. Bear half left across the field and soon there are views of Fawley Court and Temple

Almshouses in Henley churchyard.

The Angel at the end of Henley Bridge.

Island (see above). This crossfield path reaches the edge of Remenham Wood three-quarters of the way down the side of the field. Go ahead into the trees to follow the slightly winding path which cuts through a corner of the wood. (There has been some felling recently.)

Beyond the wooden stile on the far side, go half right over the sloping grass to join another path running alongside a wooden fence. Follow this path under the trees to a wooden stile. Now the faint line of the path can be seen running over the grass below the impressive house (left). Go over the stile in the far corner and along the side of a field near the low Home Farm building (left). A stile leads to a road.

Turn left to reach The Little Angel pub at the main road. Go right to walk over Henley Bridge and find The Angel.

Walk 10

MARLOW & UPSTREAM VILLAGES

———— 11 miles ————

OS Landranger 175, Pathfinder 1156 and 1157

Before pressure for the Thames Path built up in the 1970s walkers had to make a long detour away from the river on the right bank. Now the Temple Ferry crossing, which had fallen into disuse, has been replaced by a footbridge, saving 1½ miles of road route. This is a circular walk which goes up a high cliff and includes a narrow tunnel where torches are recommended. The walk starts at Marlow Station which is closed on winter Sundays. The half-way point is The Flower Pot which is also passed on Walk 9 so this can be treated as a walk into Henley.

Marlow. All Saints Church by the bridge was erected in 1835 on the site of the 12th-century church. Inside there are some memorials from the old church including one in the porch to Sir Miles Hobart which not only depicts his death but is claimed as the oldest public memorial paid by subscription. This is a popular weddings church as the confetti outside often indicates — gardener Roddy Llewellyn was married here. St Peter Street was once the main road with the bridge at the end by Old Bridge House. St Peter's, designed by Pugin of Houses of Parliament fame, has an interesting modern addition. The church has the hand of St James The Great which was once a possession of Reading Abbey upstream. The 14th-century Old Parsonage at the top of the street is Marlow's oldest house and looking down St Peter Street is Marlow Place, home of George II as Prince of Wales. The poet Shelley lived for a year at Shelley House (marked by a plaque, in West Street). Later T.S. Eliot spent about a year at the Old Post Office House nearby. The present Post Office was the house used by William Tierney Clark who designed the present famous suspension bridge based on his Hammersmith success (see page 133). This led to the Budapest commission to span the Danube. The Swiss Burger family took over the noted

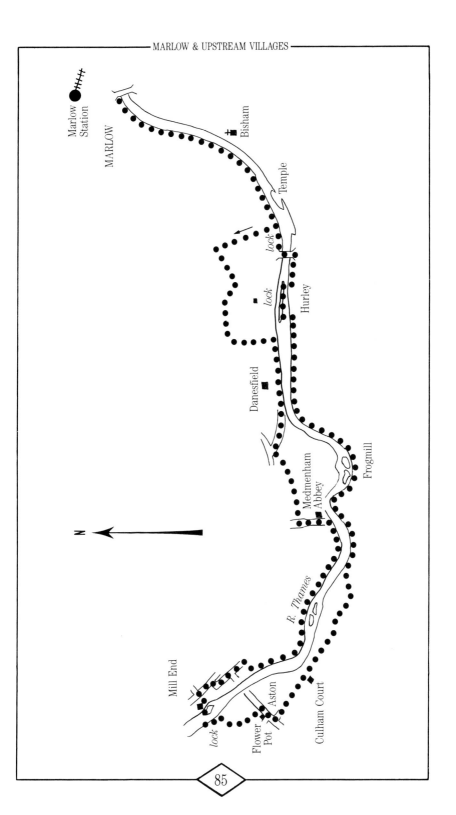

Shelley's cottage at Marlow.

bakery on the corner of Station Road and The Causeway in 1942 and despite changes the shop remains typically English with a tearoom (open daily except Sundays) and 32 different kinds of chocolate on sale along with the bread and cakes.

W. H. Smith's presence in Marlow is commendably restrained.

Leave Marlow by the park opposite Burger's and the road from the station. A path leads directly to the towpath. Bear right to walk upstream and soon there is a view over the water to Bisham church.

Bisham church. The Norman tower is the oldest part of this riverside church but, disappointingly, the door opening on to the river only dates from 1856. Buried inside is Sir Philip Hoby whose body was brought here from London by water in 1558. In later times Edward VII, as Prince of Wales, joined the Sunday congregation when staying locally.

Immediately upstream is Bisham Abbey which, like the church, is best seen from the towpath.

Bisham Abbey began as a Knights Templars house in 1139 and later became an Augustinian monastery. After the Dissolution in 1536 Henry VIII gave it to the Benedictines, who had been evicted from Chertsey Abbey downstream, to pray for the soul of Queen Jane (Seymour) but the arrangement ended in 1538. The Abbey was then granted to the divorced Anne of Cleves and passed to Sir Philip Hoby (see Bisham church above). Elizabeth I visited both as a child and in her old age. The buildings are now part of the National Sports Centre.

Bisham Church.

Bisham Abbey.

The towpath crosses several footbridges and passes through new Conservancy gates before coming level with Temple Island, known as Temple Mills papermill before the early 1980s housing. At the end of the island and within sight of the long weir, turn inland on a track running north away from Temple Lock.

The way passes through a (usually open) iron gate and runs straight ahead to an S bend at Lower Grounds Farm. Go through the gate at the side of the farm

The smart Temple footbridge opened in 1989.

Marlow Weir, Bridge and the church beyond.

buildings (left) to reach East Lodge at a T-junction.

Turn left through a broken gateway to cross a hidden wooden stile on the right of a gate. Ignore the driveway and keep ahead over the grass on the edge of Home Copse (right). Below is a riverside caravan park. At the far end go through an iron kissing gate and follow an enclosed path up to a metalled driveway leading to Harleyford Manor.

Harleyford Manor was designed by Sir Robert Taylor and built in 1755 for William Clayton. The grounds, allegedly by 'Capability' Brown, are now part of Harleyford Marine and the house is a club.

Cross the drive to go directly into a yard and then half left up steps. At the top cross a stile and turn left. Ignore any 'farm only' notices and on reaching two cottages bear right to go through a wooden gate. The gravel driveway soon bears left to Home Farm House. Keep forward on to a grass path lined on one side by evergreen trees. At the far end of the field go through the iron kissing gate.

A narrow woodland path follows the iron fence (left) downhill and then up to a T-junction by wooden gates. Go left along a narrow enclosed, path which suddenly dips down into a tunnel. At the far end there is a fine view down on to a weir at Hurley.

The path runs steeply down the cliff face to cross a stream and turn upstream by the river. The towpath is over on the right bank. Still enclosed, this left bank path runs ahead for ¼ mile to cross the stream again by a lonely cottage. Continue in the same direction along the lane whilst the river swings away to the south after Danesfield Sailing Club. Above the cliff and out of sight is Danesfield, a former RAF station seen on the return walk (see page 93). The metalled way passes a small lodge (left) and then the more substantial West Lodge (right).

On meeting a main road at once turn left up the approach to Abbey Lodge which guards a fine avenue of trees. Cross the bridge and at once bear right to an awkward iron gate. A short path winds round to a wooden stile. Go half left across the field towards the left end of a long barn. Cross another stile and go forward over a track (and probably a long-fallen tree trunk). Cross the wooden stile and bridge to continue on the (at first) enclosed path which leads to a gravel drive behind a row of cottages. Ahead is a road in Medmenham. The main village is to the right including the church and The Dog & Badger.

The walk continues to the left and before reaching the river there is the imposing entrance to Medmenham Abbey which is best seen from the right bank on the return walk.

Medmenham Abbey was a Cistercian foundation dating from 1201 and dissolved twice before the final closure in 1536. Most of the buildings including the 'ruins' are mock although there is the trace of a 13th-century pillar. The abbey became notorious in the 18th century when Sir Francis Dashwood's Hell Fire Club met here. Members called themselves the Franciscans of Medmenham and performed obscene parodies of religious rites. The motto over the door read 'Do whatever you like'. Sir Francis is also remembered as the Chancellor of the Exchequer who made a confused Budget speech which brought instant derision.

Near Medmenham.

The road leads to Medmenham Ferry. Bear right to a monument recording an historic legal victory concerning this crossing.

Medmenham Ferry Monument records an 1899 court victory to keep the ferry free for general as well as commercial use by those towing and needing to cross with the towpath. Unfortunately the ferry has long ceased to operate.

Continue upstream and beyond a Conservancy gate the way is alongside a vast open meadow which sweeps ahead round the curve of the river. Culham Court is seen to the right although it will appear on the right bank later. After a mile the towpath passes Magpie Island and enters a field below Culham Court, an isolated country house built in 1770 by an unknown architect. Continue towards a white thatched house. Do not attempt to go through the Conservancy gate into the garden but turn inland up the side of the house to a stile.

Go over this stile and a second on the left to walk down a straight lane. Soon there is a view (left) down to Aston Ferry which, being disused, means a detour to Hambledon Lock. Walk on to Mill End where the lane turns right to a main road. Go left along the main road with care. Just beyond the T-junction turn left at the far end of the white cottage. Then continue to find a narrow high-fenced path which leads to Hambledon Lock weir. Walk along the weir and over the lock gates (see page 81).

(To reach Henley turn right and follow the river for 2½ miles. Another short route to Henley begins at The Flower Pot nearby; see below.)

The walk continues downstream through the gate ahead and the larger iron gate to follow the rough lock road. Stay on the track as it turns inland towards some trees. The way winds up the hill towards The Flower Pot Inn which soon comes into view beyond a belt of trees. Where the path divides at a bend near the pub, keep ahead up a narrow footpath to Aston's Ferry Lane. Turn right for The Flower Pot.

The Flower Pot (see page 82, where there are also details of a 2-mile walk to Henley).

From the pub continue inland and (unless making for Henley) go left up a short hill to pass the entrance to Holme Farm. Where the lane bends keep forward to find an iron kissing gate. Beyond here go left to follow the top of a ridge and pass a cluster of trees (right). At once there are views down on to the river. On approaching Culham Court go over a stile and through the kissing gates which flank the vista between the mansion and the Thames.

Walk on to a wooden stile passing a field corner (left) and a walled garden. At a stile by an iron gate go on to the track which joins from the right and pass 'Horn's' (a pink cottage). Keep on the track, which runs downhill, for 200 yards to a T-junction. Climb over the stile on the left and go ahead for a few yards before

The Flower Pot at Aston.

bearing half right to the corner of the field. On the way there is a glimpse of the top of Danesfield 1½ miles away on high cliff.

Cross the footbridge guarded by stiles and follow the river bank. Inland is Lower Culham Farm below Rosehill Wood and across the water is the towpath and outward route. There are a couple more footbridges and the odd redundant stile at old field boundaries before the path and river turns north to reach (at a stile) Medmenham Ferry. Although there is an alternative path here, allowing the corner to be cut, the towpath, which has joined at the ferry, affords a very good view of Medmenham Abbey (see page 90).

The paths rejoin beyond a new stile and near the first of three islands. Go over the stile by the large Conservancy gate. The narrow rough path briefly becomes gravelled at Frogmill Farm before joining a parallel road in front of a row of well-established riverside homes. After a couple of squeeze stiles the path leaves Frogmill (and its half-hidden caravan site). Ahead is the first good view up to Danesfield with a glimpse of the smaller Whittington House and then Harleyford beyond.

Danesfield. The present magnificent mansion above the river bend was built at the turn of the century for Robert Hudson of soap fame. This was Romaine Walker's greatest design and the huge building is now occupied by the Ministry of Defence Police who took over from the RAF. Whittington, the 18th-century style house to the east and also on the cliff, was built a year before Danesfield to a design by Reginald Blomfield.

After another squeeze stile by a gate the river bends eastwards with the towpath on the edge of a wide meadow whilst opposite are high chalk cliffs with a footpath below used on the outward walk down from the tunnel beneath Whittington's grounds. On approaching Hurley Weir, Harleyford Manor can be seen downstream framed by trees. Beyond a slipway the path reaches a small iron gate and crosses a high bridge over an inlet to a boathouse. Ahead the towpath crosses the main channel. Hurley is on this right bank and can be reached by turning right before crossing the river.

Hurley. The Norman church was once part of Hurley Priory, founded in 1087. Nearby is the refectory, tithe barn and dovecote. The Olde Bell, which has a Norman doorway, was the guesthouse. Hurley Lock is said to be 'Plashwater Weir-Mill Lock' in Dickens' *Our Mutual Friend*. In 1974 the Queen sailed from here past Windsor Castle to Runnymede.

The walk continues over the arched bridge and along the metalled path on the island. Beyond the lock, cross back to the mainland on a second bridge and continue downstream. Here the path is less defined but keep near the water. On reaching a wood go over a stile. Ahead is the new bridge which replaced Temple Ferry in 1989.

The direct route back to Marlow is over the bridge and along the towpath to pass Temple Lock.

Walk 11

MAIDENHEAD & MARLOW

———— 7½ miles ————

OS Landranger 175, Pathfinder 1157

The first section of the walk is important for the view of Cliveden and its woods and makes the slightly long walk from Maidenhead Station to the town's bridge worthwhile. Later, after Cookham, the route climbs Winter Hill for good views in an area known to Kenneth Grahame who set part of *The Wind In The Willows* in the wood.

The walk starts at Maidenhead Station but a return should be booked to Marlow. Cookham has a station making it possible to break this walk in half. Cookham and Marlow Stations are closed on winter Sundays.

On leaving Maidenhead Station forecourt cross the road and turn left to go right by The Bell into Queen Street. Walk to the far end (by Boots) and go right into the High Street. Walk on the right side of the road and keep ahead over all road junctions for ⅓ mile to Maidenhead Bridge.

> **Maidenhead Bridge.** There has been a bridge here on the main London road since the mid 13th century when a hermit attached to a nearby chapel would collect the tolls. It was over an old much-repaired wooden bridge here that William of Orange crossed in 1688 to accept the Crown. The present bridge was designed by Sir Robert Taylor who was also responsible for the new Swinford Bridge above Oxford, which this resembles. Swinford retains its tolls but charges ceased here in 1903 after a public enquiry exposed misuse of revenues.

At the bridge turn left upstream and follow the road to pass the few riverside buildings. Beyond The Thames Hotel it is possible to cross the road and walk by the river. (A café is usually open in the park, left.) Ahead can be seen Boulter's Inn on the lock island.

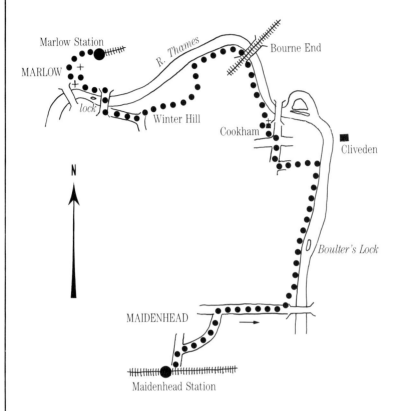

Marlow Station

MARLOW

lock

R. *Thames*

Bourne End

Winter Hill

Cookham

Cliveden

N

Boulter's Lock

MAIDENHEAD

Maidenhead Station

Boulter's Lock was once the busiest and is still the most famous thanks to such paintings as E.J. Gregory's *'Boulter's Lock — Sunday Afternoon'* which shows the lock packed with small pleasure craft in summer.

Stay on the pavement at the lock to follow the cut. After 300 yards the road leaves the river as the towpath continues ahead. At the weir the river widens and the left bank's high cliff can be fully appreciated. Along the towpath there are several substantial residences. The most impressive is the last, Islet Park House, seen as the path crosses the White Brook, which serves as an approach to the boat house.

Soon the path runs inside a line of trees and at the far end there is a first view of Cliveden on high ground ahead above the wooded grounds. Inland there are now fields and after just ½ mile the towpath comes level with Spring Cottage in the main grounds of Cliveden.

Towpath at Cliveden Reach.

Cliveden. The first house on the prime plateau site above the river was begun in 1666 for the second Duke of Buckingham. The present building is by Charles Barry of Houses of Parliament fame. William Waldorf Astor became known as 'Walled Off Astor' when he moved in declaring America to be no fit place for a gentleman. His daughter-in-law Nancy became the first woman MP and Cliveden's greatest hostess, entertaining such people as Henry James, Hilaire Belloc, Charlie Chaplin, Bernard Shaw, Lawrence of Arabia and Oswald Mosley. Churchill's comment on her crowded parties was 'thirty dishes and no damn room to eat them!' Later Cliveden was described as 'Britain's most notorious country house' after Spring Cottage featured in the Profumo Scandal. Cliveden has been let as a hotel by the National Trust but the grounds remain open to the public.

Soon the towpath switches bank at My Lady Ferry.

My Lady Ferry, the last to be operated by Thames Conservancy, continued operating until 1956. However it was not originally a passenger crossing but for the towing horses which had to be moved to the left bank for just under ½ mile before returning to the right bank to go up the Cookham Lock cut. The operation between here and Cookham Bridge involved three ferries. My Lady Ferry cottage can be seen opposite on the Cliveden estate.

Cookham Bridge tollhouse.

The way is now inland through a wood and soon the path is running parallel with a drive (right). Beyond a stile bear half left towards the white house with a high hedge. The enclosed path curves round to join Mill Lane. Turn left and follow the road into Cookham. At a junction turn right for the village centre.

Cookham. The church, scene of many weddings including actress Susan George's in 1984, has a 12th-century nave and features in Stanley Spencer's painting *'The Resurrection, Cookham'*. He was born at Fernlea in the High Street and now the Methodist church has been turned into the Stanley Spencer Gallery (open daily in summer and winter weekends). Cookham Bridge, which appears in Spencer's *'Swan Upping'*, was built in 1867 to replace the original of 1840. The toll house can be seen on the far bank. The Tea Shop at Willow Bank in the High Street is open daily.

The walk continues through the village past the main street by the Stanley Spencer Gallery (left) and Odney Lane by the Tarry Stone (right). After a few yards go left by a group of timber-framed cottages to reach the churchyard. Take the main path to the left of the church to find the river beyond a narrow kissing gate.

Turn left upstream (glancing back to see Cookham Bridge). After passing through gates at the sailing club, the towpath is along the edge of meadowland known as Cock Marsh.

Left Cookham's Tarry Stone.

Left Pub sign in Cookham refers to a traditional Thames custom.

Right *The church at Cookham.*

Below *Cookham's Stanley Spencer Gallery carries a flood warning board.*

Cookham Bridge and boatyard beyond.

Cock Marsh is one of the few remaining examples of lowland marsh areas and an exceptionally good site for wildlife which includes redshank, lapwing and wading birds. The burial mounds west of the railway are evidence of Bronze Age occupation. Rising behind the marsh is a steep chalk ridge which includes Winter Hill to the west (see below).

Beyond the gate into the National Trust area keep to the right of the belt of trees to stay on the towpath. On the far bank the River Wye (which rises in High Wycombe) can be seen entering the Thames by Andrew's Boathouses. Go through the wooden gate to pass under Bourne End Railway Bridge.

Bourne End railway bridge succeeded an 1857 wooden structure carrying a single track. This iron and steel bridge was opened in 1894 with the intention that it should be widened for a second track. However the line no longer runs to High Wycombe and only the shuttle service to Marlow remains. It is expected that a long-designed footbridge will at last be attached for the Thames Path. This crossing will then replace the disused Spade Oak Ferry (see below) where the towpath changes banks.

The towpath now runs by the gardens of several isolated residences (with no road access). Among them is The Bounty pub which predates most of the other properties and runs an irregular ferry to Bourne End. Beyond a Conservancy gate is a cattle watering spot known as The Flam. Some distance beyond another gate the path reaches a Ferry Cottage at Spade Oak Ferry which ran until 1962.

With the towpath now switched to the left bank the path here continues behind the riverside buildings and chalets. At a field corner turn left to walk south on a track crossing the large field. Climb over a stile on the far side below the amphitheatre formed by the hill and bear right up the gently-rising ledge. At first there are good views back down on to the river. Near the top of the slope the way becomes enclosed. Cross a stile by a gate and keep uphill to a road on Winter Hill.

Winter Hill, so named because it is north facing, has views across to the Chilterns but none of the Thames flowing below can be seen from here. Quarry Woods on the west side is probably the 'Wild Wood' in Kenneth Grahame's *The Wind In The Willows* explored by him as a child when living at Cookham Dean.

Turn right to a junction and right again into Gibraltar Lane — higher of the two roads. This lane bears left and runs downhill to become rough and divide. Take the left fork to pass Forest Lodge. Where the lane ends continue on a narrow woodland footpath which rises briefly before running gently downhill. Here the river can be seen below through the trees (right). The path joins the top of a lane by Quarry Clyffe House. Follow the lane downhill and just before the bottom, where the way becomes walled, there is a good view of the river bending towards Marlow. The road now runs along the edge of the river.

At a road junction go right (over a stream) with the main road and walk to the flyover 300 yards away. Climb up a flight of steps on the left (provided by the East Berkshire Ramblers). At the top turn right to walk over the road below and the Thames. On the far side of this bridge, completed in 1972, there are steps down to the towpath. Turn upstream to pass under the bridge. Use of this unpleasant concrete crossing enables one to make the traditional entry into Marlow.

Beyond a line of houses there is a grass field with at once a faint tread running away from the water. This is because before the path next becomes enclosed one must walk inland to avoid the lock. Beyond a gateway on the north side of the field turn left to follow an S bend past Marlow Mill. (But for Marlow Station go right and left at the gate.) Soon there is a magnificent view of Marlow's weir, suspension bridge and church.

After the road turns inland look out for a narrow opening in the brick wall (left). Seven Corner Alley, used by barge crews to bring horses from the lock to the towpath by the bridge, leads to St Peter Street. Turn right to pass The Two Brewers and after a few yards the alley continues to the left of The Old Malt House. The path leads into All Saints churchyard. Turn right for the Burger Tea Room (see page 84) on the corner of Station Road which leads to Marlow Station.

Marlow (see page 84).

Walk 12

WINDSOR

———4½ miles———

OS Landranger 175, Pathfinder 1173

The vast majority of visitors to Windsor never find the riverside paths. This is an easy circular route taking in the back of the Home Park, Eton College grounds and The Brocas which offers probably the very best view of the castle.

> **Windsor Castle** began as a fortress for William the Conqueror but the present impressive exterior is the result of extensive restoration by Sir Geoffrey Wyatville for George IV. St George's Chapel, in the castle precincts, was begun in 1475 and completed under Henry VIII. J.S. Stone wrote the hymn *The church's one foundation* whilst serving as curate at the nearby parish church where '*The Last Supper*' painting by Franz de Cleyn hangs after being transferred from St George's by George III. The next door Guildhall was designed by Christopher Wren with extra pillars — not actually touching the ceiling — because the council thought it looked unsafe.

There are two stations in Windsor. This walk begins at Windsor & Eton Riverside Station. Walk down Farm Yard by the station entrance to reach the river. Upstream is Windsor Bridge (see page 109). Turn right to walk downstream. Across the wide water is the weir and ahead is The Donkey House pub. Keep near the river to go through double iron gates into the narrow Romney Walk. Immediately inland is a view across the station to the Royal Waiting Room, built in 1849 to blend in with the castle above.

Continue along the Walk where in winter there are views of Eton College Chapel through the trees beyond Romney Island. At the end the route continues parallel with the river and railway (right) to reach a boatyard after passing near Romney Lock. Cross the stile on the far side of the boatyard to find the grass towpath following the river.

Where the lock island ends there is a view over to Boathouse Cottage (passed later on this walk) before passing under Black Pott's railway bridge.

Windsor Castle from the riverside.

Black Pott's Bridge was erected in 1849 to Sir Joseph Locke's design which was decorated by Sir William Tite who was making the station look regal with his Tudor Gothic theme. The bridge was slightly altered in 1892.

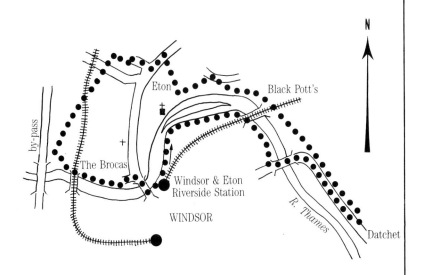

Above *Houseboat opposite The Home Park at Windsor.*

Left *Windsor Castle from the towpath.*

Victoria Bridge.

Beyond the bridge there are views of the castle and a couple of houseboats at coveted moorings on the left bank. The towpath runs directly ahead over a footbridge to the locked gates of the Home Park's private section adjoining the castle grounds. Therefore this walk leaves the river at the footbridge and bears half right to the gates at the end of the white road fence. Follow the road up on to Victoria Bridge.

> **Victoria Bridge** and its twin, Albert, downstream were erected in 1851 as successors to Datchet Bridge which lay between the two from 1706 to 1836 as replacement for a ferry. Victoria Bridge, partly designed by Prince Albert, was given a new central span in 1967.

Stay on the left-hand pavement to follow a road downhill round a curve. Soon there is a gate in the hedge (left) leading to a footpath on this route. However since this access is disputed walkers at present must continue along the pavement for 300 yards to Sumpter Mead, the first house in Datchet.

> **Datchet church** has a 13th-century chancel and the Victorian east window is a copy of the 14th-century original. Old Bridge House at the end of the High Street is a reminder of the bridge (see above). Here there is a good view over to The Home Park and a tree-lined lane once reached by ferry and featured in Shakespeare's *The Merry Wives of Windsor*.

At the side of Sumpter Mead is the entrance to a footpath. Follow this path which runs through a wood and parallel to the road (left). On meeting a track at a bend continue forward over the grass as the track swings away. At the earlier tempting gateway (left) the path joins a clearer path running ahead which serves as an access for the houseboats.

Beyond the boats (left) the way again becomes grassed. The river view is blocked by a wood which, due to a narrow backwater, is a virtual island. On approaching the railway bridge, the path is briefly enclosed before dividing. Take the left fork and walk through the low tunnel beneath the railway.

The path now runs half left to cross a footbridge. Continue ahead (not half right) to cross at stiles the fenced approach to a riverside cottage. The path now snakes through the undergrowth to a further stile. Walk across the top of a slipway where there is another view of Eton College Chapel from the riverbend. A short metalled drive leads to Boathouse Cottage by a road.

Turn left and beyond the cottage keep inside the wooden fence. Over the road there is a view north to Slough.

After a short distance turn left over a stream to enter Eton College's grounds. A gravel path runs ahead near the river (left). On reaching a brick bridge crossing a stream known as The Jordan turn away and, with the bridge behind one bear half left up the side of the cricket field towards the pavilion. Go through a kissing gate on to a road. Turn along the road which rises over The Jordan to give a magnificent view of Windsor Castle and Eton Chapel in a line. The road follows a wall, used in the St Andrew's Day Wall Game, to a junction.

Eton College was inspired by Winchester College and founded here by 19-year-old Henry VI in 1440. Seventy poor scholars formed the nucleus of the school and today there are still seventy King's Scholars although most of the school consists of 'Oppidans' who

River behind Eton College.

One of the many remarkable buildings of Eton High Street.

pay full fees. The chapel was built between 1449 and 1482 with the intention that there should be a nave added to what is really just the east end choir. Former pupils include the first Duke of Wellington, the poet Shelley, William Gladstone, Lord Snowdon and Douglas Hurd. The boys still wear black tail coats in mourning for George III.

The High Street ahead leads directly to Windsor Bridge near Windsor & Eton Riverside Station.

The walk continues to the right, past a Victorian lamp-post known as the Burning Bush, into Common Lane. Keep to the left of the 18th-century Common Lane House to pass Godolphin House (built in 1722 as a boarding house) and Holland House (left). Walk ahead along the narrow Judy's Passage. At the far end turn left for a few yards and then right on another enclosed path. A field can be seen at the end.

At the field turn sharp left and after crossing Wick Road bear half right towards the allotments against the long railway viaduct. Briefly join a metalled road and at the end of the allotments go through the fourth arch. (This is the Great Western Railway's approach to Windsor; see below). At once bear half left across a field which lies between the railway and bypass.

At a lane turn left. When the wooden fence (right) ends turn right off the lane on to a footpath which runs towards the river. Almost at once there is a view of Windsor Castle rising above the railway (left). The path joins the river by an inlet. Bear left on to the towpath and walk under Windsor's Great Western Railway Bridge on to The Brocas.

Windsor Great Western Bridge carries the branch line from Slough to Windsor. The bridge was designed by Brunel and, although this was a difficult crossing to make in one span, opened in 1849 two months ahead of the rival London & South Western Railway's line from Staines which had to cross the Thames at Black Pott's (see page 103).

After a short curve of the river there is another view of the Castle — one of the best angles and favoured by Turner — directly ahead. Over to the left looms Eton's Chapel and the more humble St Mary's in Eton High Street. Keep along the irregular natural riverbank with a changing view of the castle. On reaching the buildings (at an old ferry point) it is necessary to move inland to pass through a gateway and up a lane at the back of the Eton College Boathouse. Pass The Waterman's Arms (left) to walk up Brocas Street to Eton High Street. Turn right to walk over the bridge.

Above right
Windsor Bridge links Windsor and Eton.

Left *Windsor Bridge toll-house.*

Windsor Bridge is at least an 800-year-old crossing point. The old wooden bridge had a whipping post as late as the 17th century. Both road and river traffic paid tolls and in 1736 it was possible to walk over alive for 2d whilst being carried in a coffin would cost 6/8d. Tolls ended in 1897 after court proceedings but the toll-collector's cottage remains as part of the Old House Hotel on the Windsor side. The present 1822 bridge was the first arched iron bridge on the river. Road traffic was banned in 1970.

On the far side go left down steps on to the towpath. Farm Yard and Windsor & Eton Riverside Station are on the right.

HAMPTON COURT
& DESBOROUGH ISLAND

———— 12¼ miles ————

OS Landranger 176, Pathfinder 1190

Although this walk is outside the County of London and in Surrey, part of the left, or Middlesex, bank is now embraced by the capital. The views are mainly rural but there are encounters with the almost private world of riverside living, first on houseboats and then in the quaint 1930s' bungalows and huts. At the walk's turning point near Weybridge there are several alternatives involving a ferry and a train from Shepperton for those not tempted by the walk back.

Hampton Court Bridge. The idea of a bridge here was inspired by Walton's (see below). The very first was Chinese in appearance and levied a ½d toll on weekday walkers and a 1d on Sundays. Tolls continued in force during the time of two further structures until 1876. The toll-house is now part of The Mitre pub on the Hampton Court side. The present bridge, a little downstream from the old approach and designed by Edwin Lutyens to complement Hampton Court Palace, opened in 1933. The palace was begun by Cardinal Wolsey who described this as 'the healthiest place within twenty miles of London'. He gave the palace to Henry VIII and today its famous vine, planted in 1768, is watered by the Thames. East Molesey on the right bank is older than Hampton Court with a church, although rebuilt by the Victorians, mentioned in Domesday Book.

On leaving Hampton Court Station (which is in East Molesey) cross the road on the crossing. (Note the snack bar directly ahead which serves breakfast and other meals at non-tourist prices.) Walk across the top of Bridge Street to follow the riverside road known as River Bank.

Where the road veers inland continue ahead to the right of the war memorial. Here, beyond Molesey Lock, the towpath is known as Barge Walk. After the weir is Ash Island lined with houseboats and in the gap between Ash and Tagg's Islands is a Swiss Cottage.

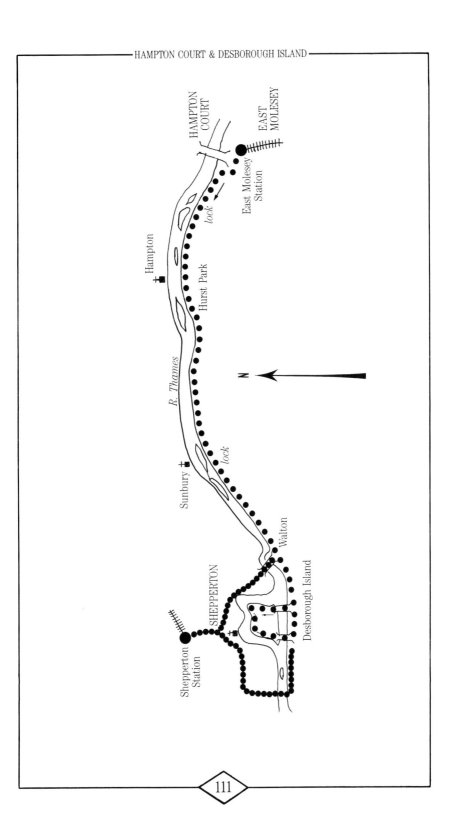

Hampton church can be reached by ferry.

Tagg's Island, named after Royal Waterman Tom Tagg, was the site of Fred Karno's leisure complex earlier this century. The Swiss Chalet on the far bank was brought here from Switzerland in 1899 and is now part of a boatyard.

Soon there is a view inland to St Paul's church spire, erected in 1888. At the entrance to East Molesey Cricket Club (flanked by the Menzies Gates) the metalled surface swings away and the towpath continues with a rough surface. After a short distance there is a brief view ahead of the domed Garrick's Temple. Soon there is a wide expanse of grass as the towpath runs by the former Hurst Park racecourse now partly covered by a Wate's estate. On approaching Garrick's Ait there is a clear view of the temple and beyond the island one is level with Hampton's church which appears to dominate the village like a cathedral.

Hampton. The large riverside church of St Mary was completed in 1831 and contains work by Eric Fraser, the *Radio Times* illustrator who lived nearby in the former home of Edward VI's midwife. During the last century most of the land surrounding the village was given over to the water industry or market gardening. The latter has disappeared whilst the Southwark & Vauxhall, Grand Junction and West Middlesex companies' waterworks have become part of the Thames Water Authority. Garrick's Temple was built in 1765 for actor Richard Garrick who lived in the house over the road. The garden is linked by a tunnel. The Hampton Ferry Boatyard, below the Bell Inn, continues to run an irregular ferry service begun in 1524.

Continue on the gravel path past the white ferry posts. The TWA waterworks are largely screened by the long Platt's Eyot where Port Hampton provides numerous facilities for passing craft and those needing winter moorings. The island's west end rises to high ground like a liner, with two bending trees providing the ship's figurehead.

Along the rising towpath are now interesting riverside homes and, down the first road, a glimpse of St Peter's, West Molesey. Then, as the river bends, the path runs below a long brick wall surrounding several reservoirs where sheep may sometimes be spotted on the inner grass slopes. On coming level with the tiny Grand Junction Island, the towpath passes between wartime defences. After another mile the wall gives way to iron railings and across the tops of the Sunbury Court Island houses is Sunbury Court mansion built in 1770 and now owned by the Salvation Army. On the towpath, level with the end of the island, is a city post. (This indicated that coal brought into London was subject to duty but today it marks the West Molesey and Walton parish boundaries.) Soon Sunbury comes into view.

Sunbury-on-Thames. The main part of the village is not seen from the towpath but the eastern end, complete with waterside pub, boatbuilders and rising buildings has the air of a seaside fishing village sometimes enhanced by seagulls. The church, dating from the Saxon period, was replaced by one designed by the Hampton Court Clerk of Works in 1752 but the main body was again rebuilt by the Victorians and has recently been greatly enlarged.

Looking across to Sunbury from the towpath.

Turk's Boatyard at Sunbury.

Walk past Sunbury Lock and, although most of the village is hidden by the Lock Ait, the church tower's cupola can be seen above the trees. The path surface is now metalled as the way passes an 1812 lock-keeper's cottage bearing the City Arms and a footbridge with cobbled ramps for horses. The Weir Hotel (left on the towpath) stands opposite the impressive Sunbury Weir. Beyond the weir the surface becomes rough as it follows the Walton Mile — an almost straight course loved by rowers and swimmers and scene of many regattas. The first island, linked to the weir, has a busy boatyard and a few 'beach hut' style living quarters for summer dwelling as well as bungalows now used as permanent homes. The second island is Wheatley's Ait.

The bridge for towing horses at Sunbury replaces an older structure.

Summerhouse near Sunbury-on-Thames.

Wheatley's Ait was used to grow osiers for basket-making until the 1880s. The first holiday residents were a group of bachelors who later allowed women to join them so long as they were off the island by midnight. Now it is a second home to sixteen families each enjoying a chalet and a share of facilities.

Ahead is not Walton Bridge but an arched crossing over Walton backwater. First the towpath reaches Walton Wharf.

Walton-on-Thames. As early as Tudor times timber was brought to the wharf to be taken downstream to London. In the last century coal was unloaded for the gas company. This reach was reserved for the watering of livestock who would sometimes be joined by elephants from a travelling circus. This is also a disused ferry and the grass approach can be seen between the residences opposite. The Anglers pub, next to the old boathouses, dominates the wharf but round the corner there is The Swan, a Young's pub. Behind both pubs and overlooking the river is River House, home of composer Sir Arthur Sullivan from 1894 to 1898. At the top of the slope from the river is another pub, the timber-framed Old Manor House, which dates from the 16th century and may have been the home of Judge Jeffreys. The last reigning Tsar of Russia stayed at Elm Grove (now council offices) at the end of the High Street in 1894 with his future wife and Prince Louis of Battenburg. The church dates from the Norman period.

The walk continues upstream to the backwater where a new bridge (1969) carries the towpath over the entry and past a chandlery. The path then joins a metalled road from the marina to pass under Walton Bridge.

Walton Bridge is probably the least attractive on the river although the first, painted by Canaletto, was an unusual wooden geometrical design. This was opened in 1750 as a result of a wealthy commuter wanting to use the Middlesex road into London. The second bridge was erected in 1783 and painted by Turner. A third, Victorian, structure was damaged in the Second World War and gave way to the present 'temporary' Bailey Bridge.

Beyond the bridge, the towpath is over the grass of Cowey Sale with a road running parallel nearby. Ahead the river divides giving navigation a choice between the old channel and the man-made cut under the bridge. Climb up the steps on to the bridge for a fine view back to Walton Bridge round the bend and, westwards, up Desborough Cut.

Desborough Cut. Over a century after the cut was first suggested (and supported by the Grand Old Duke of York living at nearby Oatlands) work began in 1930. This new channel created a large island which has been preserved as a rural oasis.

Cross the bridge on to Desborough Island and where the road swings left keep near the water on a drive marked 'Brownacres' (leading to land owned by a Mr Brown in the 1930s and now a rugby club). Beyond the Brownacres gateway (left) the towpath runs ahead. At first there is little river view as the way snakes

Shepperton from Desborough Island.

through the trees (and maybe over a fallen trunk). Soon the path runs near the river as the bank turns south. On entering Point Meadow (forming the island's western end) there is an 1861 City post. From the towpath there is now a clear view of Shepperton Manor and the village nestling around the church.

Shepperton means 'shepherds' habitation' and once belonged to Westminster Abbey. There was a church here in Norman times but it was rebuilt in James I's reign following a severe flood — the Thames was then tidal as far as Staines. The tower was added in 1710 and inside the tiny building are early Victorian box pews. The church, dedicated to St Nicholas the patron saint of sailors, has a partly Tudor rectory and stands on the north side of a charming village square. Mainly 18th-century buildings back on to the river including two pubs once frequented by stars filming at nearby Shepperton Studios. Ferry Cottage in the village is a reminder that there was once a ferry here.

Turn away from the Shepperton view to follow the island's west bank. After a short distance there is another City post (left). A flooded gravel pit can be seen on the mainland. Just before the tip of the island take the left fork up to a bridge spanning Desborough Cut. On the bridge's upstream side there is a plaque unveiled by Lord Desborough and a view of D'Oyly Carte Island.

Shepperton Ferry.

D'Oyly Carte Island, formerly Folly or Silly Eyot, was intended as an annex to The Savoy but a year before the hotel in The Strand opened planning permission for the island was refused. The new building became Richard D'Oyly Carte's home instead and visitors included William S. Gilbert and Sir Arthur Sullivan. Access was then not by bridge but a ferry which was summoned by ringing a bell by the towpath.

D'Oyly Carte Island.

Walk down the steps from the Desborough bridge to reach the towpath. (To visit Shepperton, where there is a station, walk upstream past D'Oyly Carte Island to Shepperton Ferry which runs at least hourly across to Shepperton Ferry Lane. At the far end go right for the village square, then up Church Road and left into the High Street to find the station. But to rejoin the walk at Walton Bridge do not go into the High Street but ahead into Russell Road and right into Walton Lane.)

The main walk continues downstream along the almost straight Desborough Cut towpath to rejoin the outward route.

Hampton Court can be reached in about two hours. Walking eastwards new vistas are opened up especially at Sunbury and on approaching Platt's Eyot there is a view of the suspension bridge on its north side and an early sighting of Garrick's Temple.

RICHMOND

―――――5 miles――――

OS Landranger 176, Pathfinder 1174

Richmond is the base for an easy circular walk along the towpath past a village, a working ferry and a couple of stately homes to the largest urban park in Britain. Richmond is noted for its teashops and restaurants such as Mrs Beeton's on Hill Rise (open daily and at the end of the walk) and Café Mozart in Church Court. In Richmond Park the route passes through the grounds of Pembroke Lodge where there is a café.

The walk starts at Richmond Station.

Richmond-upon-Thames was West Sheen until Henry VII called his palace here after one of his titles derived from Yorkshire. Mary and Philip of Spain chose Richmond for their honeymoon and when Elizabeth I died here her ring was dropped from the gateway and taken by horse to James VI in Edinburgh. The last monarch to live at the palace was Charles I whose chaplain founded the almshouses in The Vineyard after the King's execution. Actor Edmund Kean is buried in the parish church. A blue plaque in Paradise Street marks the house where Leonard and Virginia Woolf founded the Hogarth Press on the kitchen table. Although a London Borough, Richmond retains a country town atmosphere and its recent riverside development is a neo-classical shops and office complex by Quinlan Terry.

On leaving Richmond Station turn left and follow the main street round a bend to Dickens & Jones. Here go ahead down Water Lane at the side of the Post Office. The narrow cobbled road runs down into the river by The White Cross Hotel. At the river bear left along the towpath to pass Richmond's much praised neo-classical development (see above). Ahead is Richmond Bridge.

Right *Looking through the gatehouse of Richmond Palace.*

Below *Richmond's new riverside development.*

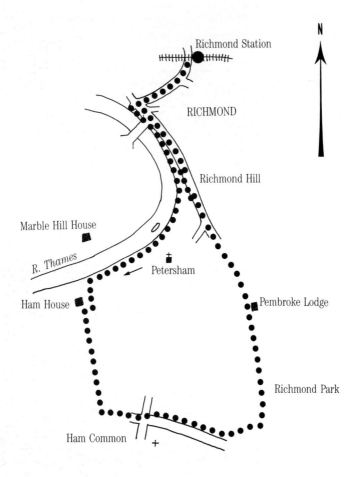

Richmond Station

RICHMOND

Richmond Hill

N

Marble Hill House

R. Thames

Petersham

Ham House

Pembroke Lodge

Richmond Park

Ham Common

Richmond Bridge, the oldest on the Thames in London, replaced a ferry in 1777. Tolls were levied until the last shareholder died in 1859. Pedestrians paid ½d to cross but would be asked for 1d if pushing a wheelbarrow. The bridge, which was painted by Turner, was widened by 12 ft in 1937.

Beyond the bridge is the Captain Webb cruising hotel mooring and Richmond Pier. The river is still tidal here and the towpath is liable to occasional flooding between here and The Three Pigeons where the path briefly moves away from the river to higher ground. Unless there is flooding do not go ahead through the swing gate on to Petersham Meadows. Instead bear right back to the riverside.

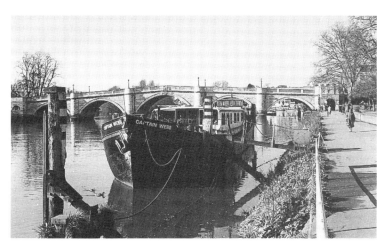

Above *The Captain Webb floating hotel at its moorings above Richmond Bridge.*

Right *Part of a boatyard at Richmond.*

Here one can look up to the top of Richmond Hill which is reached towards the end of this walk (see page 128). On the river near Glover's Island there may still be the raft of the local hermit who has long defied Port of London regulations by living on the water. The towpath is bounded by Petersham Meadows as far as the Petersham slipway at the end of River Lane.

Petersham. The church seen across the meadows has a partly Norman chancel, box pews and a gallery which give an 18th-century feel. The Queen Mother's parents were married in the church in 1881. Outside George Vancouver, the discoverer of Vancouver Island, is buried by the churchyard's south wall. Until 1982 cows grazed the meadows for the Express Dairies and the new farmer, who keeps sheep and goats, is keen to restore the dairy tradition.

Continue along the towpath and after ¼ mile there is a direct view over the water to Marble Hill House standing on a vast lawn.

Marble Hill House is a Palladian villa built for George II's mistress, Lady Suffolk, in the 1720s. Mrs Fitzherbert, the Prince Regent's wife, lived there in 1795. The interior restoration has been compared with Wilton House and Versailles.

150 yards further on there are the landing steps for Hammerton's Ferry (founded

On Petersham Meadows cows have given way to goats.

Hammerton's ferry.

in 1914) which runs daily across to Marble Hill. Here at the ferry leave the towpath by turning left on to a footpath. After a few yards bear half right (there may be a broken gateway) towards the corner of Ham House.

Ham House is a National Trust property run by the Victoria & Albert Museum. Built in 1610, the mansion is much as the Earl of Lauderdale and his wife Elizabeth Dysart would have known it from about 1672 when they married at Petersham church. In 1678 John Evelyn wrote that Ham 'is indeed inferior to few of the best villas in Italy itself; the House furnished like a great Prince's; the Park with Flower Gardens, Orangeries, Groves, Avenues, Courts, Statues, Perspectives, Fountains, Aviaries and all this at the banks of the sweetest River in the World, must needs be admired.' Later Horace Walpole wrote: 'It is so blocked up and barricaded with walls, vast trees, and gates, that you think yourself a hundred years back . . .'. In 1976 the garden was restored to its 17th-century design which resembles a Union Jack. Open daily except Mondays; admission £2 (concessions £1). During the summer teas are served in the garden which is open free.

Except for viewing purposes do not cross the front of Ham House but walk up the avenue at the side — horses tend to keep to the left here leaving a smooth path for walkers. Halfway along there is a view of the back of Ham House and its new garden through wrought iron gates. At a T-junction turn right for another view of the garden at a gateway. Here one should turn away from the house and follow the now less formal south drive for ½ mile (crossing a road on the way) to Ham Common.

Ham. Cardinal Newman said that when he dreamt of heaven he saw Ham. His childhood was spent at Newman House in Ham Street where he remembered the windows illuminated with candles in 1805 to celebrate Nelson's victory at Trafalgar. The church, beyond Upper Ham Road, has the tomb of Violet Hyacinth Bowes-Lyon who died before her sister, The Queen Mother, was born. Their mother had been married from Forbes House (now rebuilt) on the west side of the Common.

Bear left at the Common and, ignoring two turnings to the left, follow the road to a crossroads. Over to the left beyond the bus shelter is The New Inn. Cross the main road into Ham Gate Avenue. The first cottage is Sudbrook Cottage, home of the late Beverley Nicholls and a little further on is the impressive early 18th-century Ormerley Lodge where the Prince Regent and Mrs Fitzherbert spent part of their honeymoon.

A clear path runs under the trees and along the side of the straight road for ½ mile to reach Park Gate House at the entrance to Richmond Park.

Richmond Park is the remains of Shene Chase which Charles I enclosed in 1637. The roads remain unfenced although traffic has recently built up to such levels that there is concern it may be having an effect on the 600 red and fallow deer. In 1988 the rutting season was inexplicably delayed. This is a Royal Park and by tradition the Queen supplies venison to the Archbishop of Canterbury, the Lord Mayor of London and the Prime Minister. There are several lodges in the park including White Lodge built for George II and now the Royal Ballet School. Queen Mary spent her childhood at the house and her son, the Duke of Windsor, was baptised there. Princess Alexandra lives at Thatched House Lodge which was built for Sir Robert Walpole, the first Prime Minister.

On entering the park at once leave the road and bear half left past the pond (and toilets) to follow the path up the steep slope. At the top turn left to follow the path known as Hornbean Walk along the top of the ridge. There are views down into the river valley. At one point the path goes over a large hump by a tree before running near a road. On approaching a fenced area, shrouded in trees and bushes, try the gate (bolted against the deer) to enter the grounds of Pembroke

Lodge. (If the gate is locked follow the boundary ahead to the front gate.) Inside the grounds a path leads ahead to the house.

Pembroke Lodge began as Molecatchers Cottage and was enlarged for the Countess of Pembroke who died here in 1831. The house was then lent to William IV's daughter Elizabeth Fitzclarence whose mother was an actress. Later Queen Victoria invited her Prime Minister Lord John Russell to live here and he enlarged the house again. His grandson Bertrand Russell spent much of his childhood here. During the Second World War it was used by SOE when officers included David Niven. There is a good view from the back of the building and the tearoom inside is open daily.

Go along the back of the house to pass below Henry VIII's Mound (where the King is said to have waited for a signal from the Tower confirming Anne Boleyn's execution).

Walk through the laburnham tunnel and just before the James Thomson memorial there is, below the bank, a view down on to an ice-house. Go through the Lodge gate to follow the way ahead to the Richmond Park gate. Continue past the Star & Garter Home to reach the famous Thames viewpoint at the top of Richmond Hill.

Pembroke Lodge in Richmond Park.

View from Richmond Hill.

Richmond Hill. The view downstream from the river bend towards Marble Hill beyond Glover's Island has been attempted by numerous artists including Peter de Wint, Turner and Walter Sickert. Sir Joshua Reynolds lived at Wick House and saw this view daily. Virginia's Richmond took its name from here after a tobacco farmer was reminded of a view of the River James as he stood on this spot.

To reach the town centre continue ahead along a descending path parallel to the road. On joining the road keep downhill to pass the tiny Continental Patisserie teashop (open daily) on the right and Mrs Beeton's (see page 120).

Walk 15

PUTNEY'S BOAT RACE COURSE

——— 8 miles ———

OS Landranger 176, Pathfinder 1175

This circular route follows almost the entire Universities' Boat Race course rowed every spring. The outward route weaves in and out of little-known riverside paths with good views of the rural 'Surrey' bank. The turning point at Barnes is reached in about two hours and the more direct return on the towpath takes a little less although the interest is increased as one looks across the water to missed wharves and just-explored paths. In winter gulls can be seen swooping at low tide and there is an abundance of plant life along the towpath — step off the path and you can be covered in burrs within sight of Hammersmith Town Hall. There are plenty of pubs and transport at Hammersmith and Barnes. The walk starts at Putney Bridge Station.

On leaving Putney Bridge Underground station cross the road (Ranelagh Gardens) to walk down the side of the railway bridge. Do not bear left under the bridge but go forward on to a new path leading to the riverside in front of Carrara Wharf.

A bridge carries the path over a drawdock (or boat launching point) where there is a view inland to The Eight Bells in Fulham High Street. This is where the original Putney Bridge met the Fulham bank. The path continues in front of Swanbank Court (on the site of Swan Wharf once occupied by a brewery) to pass under Putney Bridge.

Putney Bridge. A temporary pontoon bridge was thrown across here during the Civil War by the Roundheads but the first real bridge to replace the ferry was a wooden structure completed in 1729. For twenty years until Westminster Bridge opened this was the only Thames bridge between London Bridge and Kingston. A week after the opening of Putney's new bridge, the Prince of Wales crossed on his way to a hunt at Richmond and gave the toll-keepers a generous £5. The present bridge was erected in 1884 a little upstream of the first which was approached from either Fulham High Street or just in front of Putney church.

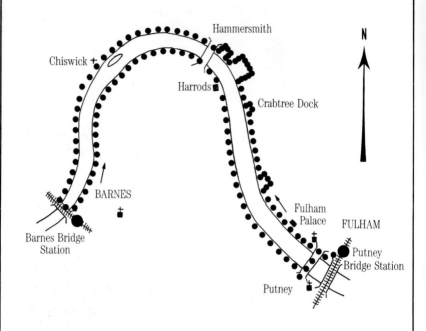

The tunnel under the bridge leads into Bishop's Park.

> **Bishop's Park** is made up of the grounds of Fulham Palace, official residence of the Bishop of London from Norman times until 1973 when the diocese purchased a small house in Westminster. The present Palace dates from the 16th century and is now owned by the local council. All Saints church, long associated with the Palace, has a medieval tower under the 1845 refacing and numerous monuments. Ten bishops are buried in the churchyard.

Turn to the left to reach the riverside path where there is a view of Putney Pier and the boathouses on the far bank. The luminous post downstream of the pier marks the Boat Race start. The path, overhung with plane trees, runs ahead for over ½ mile to where (to avoid Fulham Football Ground) the way turns inland to meet Stevenage Road. Go left to pass the front of the football ground.

> **Fulham Football Ground** is known as Craven Cottage after the thatched house of that name which stood here from about 1780 until a fire in 1888. The villa had Egyptian styled interiors and now the present Craven Cottage, seen by the gates, is used as offices by the club.

Right *Swan Wharf drawdock at Fulham.*

Below *All Saints, Fulham at the end of Putney Bridge.*

The intricate brickwork at Fulham Palace.

At the end of the football ground go left up a narrow path into Stevenage Park residential development to rejoin the river. From this high path, where the buildings are set back, there are good views and already Harrods Depository can be seen upstream on the far side (see page 138). The path crosses a Shell petrol depot wharf (where gates may be closed during off-loading from barges). Hammersmith Bridge (see below) comes into view and, just before a sunken playground, the Boat Race mile marker is visible on the opposite bank.

The path narrows, briefly rises at steps, and bears inland to Crabtree Dock — now dominated by The Crabtree Tavern but a former boatbuilder's yard is still visible. Go ahead into Rainville Road and turn left to pass the front of the pub and Palace Wharf. At Dorset Wharf go left to rejoin the river. The path passes a residential and business development before reaching Thames Wharf, home of the noted River Café.

River Café started out as the Thames Wharf studios' staff canteen but at the end of 1988 (when a meal cost around £21) it was declared to be *The Times* Italian Restaurant of the Year. The restaurant, open weekdays only and said to serve even better Italian food than many restaurants in Italy, has tables outside in warm weather. One of the proprietors is architect Richard Rogers whose models can be seen through the windows next door.

Continue to Thames Reach where there is a good view of Harrods. Here one must turn inland for the moment although development plans will eventually continue the riverside path.

Walk up Colwith Road and go left at the crossroads into Rannoch Road. Keep ahead to a T-junction. Here, go right and then left at Newspaper House to follow Distillery Road. At Chancellors Road go left back to the river and continue upstream along Chancellors Wharf.

Chancellors Wharf. Rent from a meadow near here went to the Chancellor of St Paul's Cathedral in the 12th century. On the south end of this site stood Brandenburgh House named after the Margrave of Brandenburgh-Anspach who entertained lavishly here between 1792 and 1806. Queen Caroline died here the following year just after being refused entry to her estranged husband George IV's Coronation in 1821. It was largely thanks to a massive demonstration of support by watermen on the river outside the house that moves against the Queen were dropped. Soon after her death the house was demolished.

At the end of the new path it is necessary to turn inland to skirt the Riverside Studios art centre (a former film studio owned by Jack Buchanan) by way of Crisp Road and Queen Caroline Street which leads to a drawdock. Follow the path under Hammersmith Bridge.

Hammersmith Bridge. William Tierney Clark's 1820s' suspension bridge seen in Walter Greaves' *'Hammersmith Bridge on Boat Race Day'* painting was replaced in the 1880s by Joseph Bazalgette who re-used some of the materials and built new iron towers with heraldic decoration. A suspension bridge was popular because it caused less obstruction than the usual arched bridge and Tierney Clark went on to build Marlow's suspension bridge (see page 84). He is buried in St Paul's, Hammersmith (by the flyover), where his memorial stone bears the outline of a suspension bridge.

The walk continues along the riverside Lower Mall where the 18th-century houses include the home of the London Transport Rowing Club. The Blue Anchor pub opened in 1720. The way leads to Furnival Gardens by Hammersmith Pier.

Hammersmith Pier. Furnival Gardens was created in 1936 over a creek which once ran back to King Street and around which Hammersmith village developed. A typical old street survives by The Dove (see below), a 17th-century coffee house turned pub which appears as 'The Pigeons' in A.P. Herbert's novel *The Water Gipsies*. Customers have included Charles II, Nell Gwynne, J.M.W. Turner and James Thomson who wrote the words for *'Rule Britannia'* upstairs.

Go up the alley behind the houses ahead to pass first the house where T.J. Cobden-Sanderson founded the Doves Press (left and marked by a blue plaque) and The Dove. The road opens out in front of Kelmscott House (right) which faces the river.

Kelmscott House was the home of William Morris, the designer and craftsman, who bought the house from the poet George Macdonald in 1878. Earlier it had been the home of electric telegraph inventor Francis Ronald. Morris changed the name of the house from 'The Retreat' to 'Kelmscott' after his country home, also on the Thames, near Lechlade. He and Emery Walker (see below) ran the Kelmscott Press from the room above the garage. William Morris died here in 1896.

Once more there is a river view. Continue where the road ends. (Oil Mill Lane recalls Albert Mills here where oil seeds were processed at the turn of the century.) Beyond the short arcaded walk, the way bends to pass The Old Ship pub.

The Old Ship dates from the 16th century although much of the house was rebuilt in Battle of Waterloo year, 1815. The front door was moved to the south side on Jubilee Day 1977 just before the pub was declared 'Pub of The Year'.

Follow the path into Hammersmith Terrace where the houses still retain their exclusive riverside gardens.

Left *Hammersmith Bridge.*

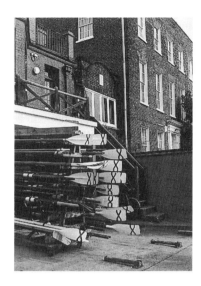

Right *Kelmscott House, home of William Morris, at Hammersmith.*

Hammersmith Terrace. A.P. Herbert, who lived at numbers 12 and 13, was President of the Black Lion Skittles Club until his death in 1971. Calligrapher Edward Johnston designed the Johnston typeface for London Transport whilst living at number 3. When he moved here in 1905 houses could easily be rented for £60 a year and Johnston considered it had the advantages of town and country combined. Sir Emery Walker made way for Johnston by moving up to number 7 where the Walker blue plaque has been placed. However it was at number 3 that Walker, who worked with Morris (see above), helped in the founding of the Doves Press (see above).

Beyond the Eyot Corner Shop the riverside houses cease and give way to gardens belonging to houses on the right. Island House and its neighbours have discreet flood defences for here the water often covers the road at high tide. Also here the road is level with an island.

Chiswick Eyot is the home of Canada geese, ducks and herons. The willows, which strengthen the land against erosion, were once used to make fish baskets. Today local residents sometimes saw up drift wood for their fireplaces.

Overlooking the island are beautiful Chiswick period houses including Strawberry and Walpole Houses which open their gardens annually under the National Gardens scheme.

A Chiswick resident collecting driftwood.

Walpole House, partly 16th-century, was home of Barbara Villiers, Duchess of Cleveland who bore Charles II three children. The house is named after the first prime minister's relatives who lived here. Later it became a school where boarders included Thackeray who may have used the setting for the Academy in *Vanity Fair*.

The road leads directly to a junction with Chiswick Draw Dock and the church.

Chiswick church is dedicated to St Nicholas, patron saint of sailors, and has a 15th-century tower. Artist William Hogarth is buried outside the south wall. (His house, beyond the nearby Hogarth Roundabout at the end of Church Street, is open to the public.) On the north side of the church, Powell's Walk leads to a large cemetery where artist James McNeil Whistler (who lived on the Chelsea riverside) is buried to the right of the gates. On the west side of the path running south from Whistler's grave is the grave of Henry Joy, Lord Lucan's Staff Trumpeter, the man who sounded the Charge of the Light Brigade.

Fishing at Barnes.

There is a walkway leading from the side of the dock but at present this riverside path has no exit so the walk continues ahead up the, at first narrow, Chiswick Walk which runs along the back of Church Wharf. (This may be developed by the end of the 1990s.) At the far end the road bears right to a junction.

Go sharp left down a private road marked as a cycleway. At the far end bear left with a metalled path to the river. This is also the cycleway but after a short distance a less well-defined path branches off to run even nearer the riverbank. Inland there is a large sports field and across the river a fine view of Barnes. Just before Barnes Bridge the path crosses the front of a boathouse. Take the steps ahead up to the footbridge attached to the railway bridge.

Barnes Bridge dates from 1846 and when the footbridge was attached in the 1890s it was made to withstand the Boat Race crowds. Unfortunately they have no view of the finish which is a short distance upstream at Mortlake.

On the far side steps lead down to the Barnes Bridge Station entrance. Go right to walk downstream. Among the houses here is number 10 where composer

Gustav Holst lived from 1908-13. Next to The Waterman's Arms and The Bull's Head is Barnes High Street.

Barnes church has recently been rebuilt after a disastrous fire in which the 16th-century tower survived with its clock in working order. The church had been consecrated by Archbishop Langton on his way back from securing King John's assent to Magna Carta upstream at Runnymede. Opposite the pond is the village's oldest house, Millbourne House, where novelist Henry Fielding lived from 1748 to 1752. Behind the Georgian façade is an Elizabethan fireplace and Jacobean stairs.

The walk continues past the two riverside pubs. At some point here cross the road to join the pavement which, as the towpath, is soon left by the river as the road veers inland.

For a short distance there is a double path by a flood wall. Over the next 1½ miles the way is wooded with few buildings by the river and good views of the outward walk through Chiswick. Opposite Chiswick Draw Dock there are steps for the disused ferry. Just beyond Chiswick Eyot can be seen the tower of St Peter's, familiar to drivers on the Great West Road. At one point there is a view inland across to Harrods Depository which reminds one of the degree of riverbend at Hammersmith. On approaching Hammersmith Bridge there is a view across to the tower of St Paul's, Hammersmith, completed in 1889 and the resting place of the bridge's designer (see page 133).

Pass under Hammersmith Bridge. Soon the towpath crosses the remains of the railway line linking Harrods with the wharf.

Harrod's Depository so resembles the Knightsbridge store that on Boat Race day television viewers are sometimes confused when the commentator speaks of the crews 'passing Harrods'. The main building was erected in 1894 on the site of a candle factory and families returning from the Empire would store furniture here and stay in a flat at the back of the Knightsbridge shop whilst looking for a permanent home. Today orders taken at Brompton Road are often despatched direct from the Depository.

Further round the bend, the lonely Boat Race mile post indicates that Putney is not far away. The boundary of Putney is marked by Beverley Brook which rises on Wimbledon Common and was once the Surrey county boundary. This is also the start of the towpath which ends at the Tunnel House in Gloucestershire (see page 14).

The Beverley Brook footbridge leads on to a fine promenade running past the boathouses. Rising above Putney Bridge on a clear day is the flashing Crystal Palace radio mast seven miles away. Just beyond Putney Pier is the start of the

View of Harrod's Depository from Crabtree Dock.

Boat Race marked by a stone and the initials 'UBR'. Walk towards Putney church, dwarfed by the ICL building.

Putney church. The 15th-century church tower was refaced in 1837 just before All Saints, opposite, received the same treatment. The church has been dramatically and successfully reordered following a fire which fortunately did not affect the Bishop West Chapel. West was a local baker's son who became Bishop of Ely and Catherine of Aragon's chaplain during her divorce proceedings. A recent plaque records the Putney Debates chaired by Cromwell in this church when it is said that the male participants sat round the altar with their hats on. This discussion of democratic principles influenced the drafting of the US Constitution over a century later. The historian Edward Gibbon was baptised here in 1737 and other visitors included Samuel Pepys who left his hat under a pew and Charles Dickens who set David Copperfield's wedding here. Open weekdays 10 to noon.

To reach Putney Bridge underground station cross the bridge. Steps lead down to the subway from the upstream side. Either retrace the outward route along the river to the railway bridge or go directly ahead to the back of the draw dock and into Ranelagh Gardens to find the station.

Walk 16

DOCKLANDS

──── 5½ miles ────

OS Landranger 177, Pathfinder 1159 and 1175

Docklands is the greatest contrast to the upper reaches which have more in common with the estuary, for here there are few trees, little grass and not many birds. But this is a fascinating area with an ever-changing waterfront whose new developments are providing exciting new riverside paths. There is much to see and this circular walk should be an all-day outing but thanks to handy transport, including the River Bus service and Docklands Light Railway, the route can easily be broken off and taken up again later.

The walk starts at Tower Bridge's north end near Tower Hill (LT), Tower Gateway (DLR) and Fenchurch Street (BR) Stations.

> **Tower Bridge**, designed by Sir John Wolfe Barry, was completed in 1894.

On the north side of Tower Bridge look for the steps leading down to the bank and walk downstream past the new but already much photographed 'Girl with a Dolphin' fountain erected in 1973. Opposite is Butler's Wharf (see page 153). Go ahead to cross the drawbridge over the St Katharine Dock entrance.

> **St Katharine Dock** was opened in 1828 after 11,300 people had been evicted from the site to make way for the basin and two docks where ivory, marble, wine, tea and turtles were unloaded. The Dock closed in 1968 and the huge 826-bedroom Tower Thistle Hotel opened in 1973 with the Historic Ship Collection following in 1979. The name St Katharine recalls the hospital for thirteen poor persons founded here by Queen Matilda in 1148. It survived the Reformation and continues as the Royal Foundation of St Katharine in Butcher Row (see page 145) where the chapel incorporates the 14th-century stalls from the original chapel which stood just beyond the present Dock entrance.

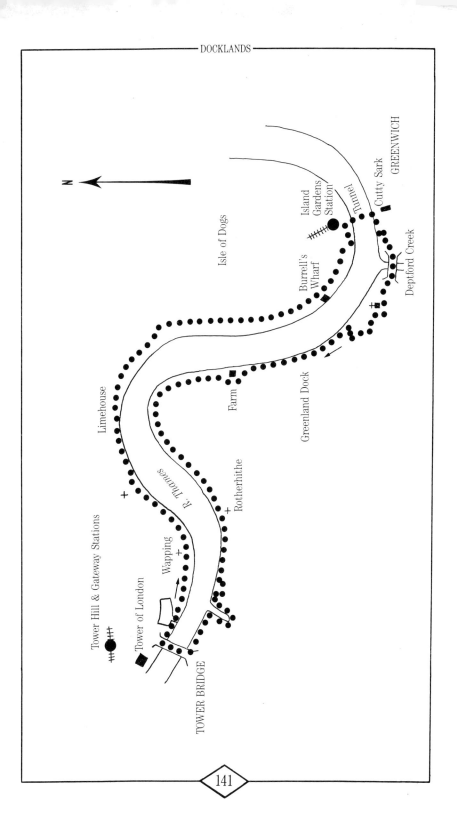

The Pool of London.

Turn right to pass the Nore lightship which once guarded the Thames estuary. Bear right again to leave the Dock and enter St Katharine's Way. On the right is President's Quay, home of the RNVR since 1988 when HMS *President* by the Embankment was sold. Just after a junction the road crosses the former entrance to London Western Docks, now partly covered by News International (*The Times, The Sunday Times, The Sun* and *The News of the World*). Across the river there is a view up St Saviour's Dock (see page 153).

Continue along the cobbled Wapping High Street which looks nothing like a typical high street and a scene of slow but great change. The road rises slightly to enter Wapping at Wapping Pierhead.

Wapping Pierhead is the original entrance to London Docks dug in 1805 with the two terraces of houses for dock officials added in 1811–13. The entrance was filled in following the closure of the docks in 1969.

Continue ahead to pass Wapping Old Stairs by The Town of Ramsgate public house.

The Town of Ramsgate changed its name from The Red Cow due to the habit of Ramsgate fishermen landing their catches at Wapping Old Stairs where Judge Jefferies was captured in 1688 trying to escape to Hamburg. During the last century convicts were chained in the pub cellar before deportation to Australia. Oliver's Wharf next door, built in the 1870s and used as a tea warehouse, was one of the first of Wapping's many conversions into flats.

View upstream to Tower Bridge from Wapping Pierhead.

Opposite is the churchyard of St John's — only the 18th-century tower remains alongside the former school which has interesting decoration over the doors in Scandrett Street. A little further on Waterside Gardens allows a view of the river and St James's, Bermondsey — a Waterloo church much admired by Sir John Betjeman. Wapping Police Station is the headquarters of the river police founded in 1789 in advance of the Metropolitan Police. Soon Wapping High Street runs between high warehouses to a junction with Wapping Lane, the heart of Wapping.

Old school entrance at Wapping.

Wapping High Street was crowded in Elizabethan times when the marshland to the north was drained under Dutch supervision. With the coming of the docks, the village became an island reached only by drawbridges. St Peter's in Wapping Lane opened in 1866 on the eve of a serious cholera outbreak. This pioneer Anglo-Catholic church still maintains the St Peter's Day procession around the parish despite a dwindling population. This was the first place in Britain to have the fuchsia after a gardener bought the plant from a sailor just back from the West Indies.

Continue along the High Street to pass the Underground Station which uses Brunel's shaft. (For a short cut take the tube one stop south to Rotherhithe; see page 151). The walk continues past new developments to bear left into Garnet Street. After a short distance turn right into Wapping Wall. At the far end is The Prospect of Whitby.

The Prospect of Whitby dates from 1520 as the board outside listing the Kings and Queens indicates but the name was only introduced in 1777 when *Prospect*, a Whitby-registered ship, moored in the river long enough to become a local feature. Customers have included painter J.M.W. Turner and, it is claimed, the sailor who sold the fuchsia (see above).

Bear left with the road at Prospect Wharf and leave Wapping by crossing the 1930s' bridge which once lifted to allow ships to enter Shadwell Basin. Ahead can be seen St Mary's, Cable Street, and above the dock is St Paul's, Shadwell, which is also known as 'The Sea Captain's Church'. After a short distance turn right up an enclosed path leading to Shadwell's King Edward Park. The round building is a ventilation shaft for the Rotherhithe Tunnel.

King Edward Memorial Park was opened by George V in 1922 on the site of the Shadwell Fish Market. A plaque recalls the voyage of Sir Martin Frobisher from here in Elizabeth I's reign.

The path continues ahead in front of the Free Trade Wharf.

Free Trade Wharf was once an East India Company store built in 1795 with numerous additions. As recently as the 1970s Dutch coasters berthed here. The arms of the East India Company remain above The Highway entrance to the new development where there are preserved railway lines outside the shops.

The 'Sea Captains' Church at Shadwell Basin.

The riverside path joins Narrow Street by way of a path inland behind Keepier Wharf.

Keepier Wharf, built in 1830, was a coal depot and takes its name from a coal-mining area in County Durham. On the east side is Ratcliffe Cross Stairs and directly north in Butcher Row is the Royal Foundation of St Katharine (see page 140).

Continue up Narrow Street which has a few riverside paths but several 'windows' on the Thames. The first is from the bridge over the Limehouse Basin entrance where the Regent's Canal joins the river. The next bridge is over the disused entrance to Limehouse Cut. (It was here that the SDP 'Gang of Four' stood to launch the 'Limehouse Manifesto' in 1981.) Beyond Hough's Wharf and the new Blyth's Wharf development is The Grapes.

The Grapes is said to be 'The Six Jolly Fellowship Porters' in Dickens' *Our Mutual Friend*. It had an unenviable reputation for getting its customers drunk and then rowing them out into the Thames to be tipped out and then recovered drowned ready to be sold for anatomy experiments. The older houses next door date from the Elizabethan period.

To the left is The House They Left Behind pub. Keep forward and at junction turn right into Three Colt Street.

Three Colt Street, Limehouse, is named after an 18th-century pub. Then the street was known as Limehouse Corner for this is the original 'Limehouse' where kilns were in operation in the 14th century. Hidden behind the buildings is an inlet on the river bend known as Limehouse Dock.

Left *A surviving pub in Limehouse.*

Right above *The Cascades development seen from Durand's Wharf.*

Walk on as the street changes its name to Emmett Street and turn left to go down Bowley Street. Now turn right to follow West Ferry Road. At first there are signs of much change as this is the edge of the controversial Canary Wharf development which embraces the riverside as well as the middle of the West India Docks. Soon the road passes the equally controversial Cascades flats (right) condemned by Prince Charles. Shortly afterwards the road crosses the old West India Docks western entrance which created the Isle of Dogs.

Isle of Dogs was so called before becoming a real island in 1805 when the West India Dock was linked to the east side. The name may refer to Henry VIII's kennels which were here. Earlier the sparsely inhabited area had been known as Stepney Marsh.

A short distance ahead is Cuba Street leading (right) to a River Bus pier.

Follow West Ferry Road past the shopping centre opposite Sir John McDougall Gardens (named after the self-raising flour inventor who had a granary nearby) which affords an excellent view of Surrey Docks. The road bends to cross the old Millwall Docks entrance by *The Daily Telegraph* printworks. Beyond here short stretches of riverside path are being constructed as part of new developments such as Cyclops Wharf. The Vulcan pub (right) marks the former entrance to Deptford Ferry Road which leads to the ferry point for Deptford (see page 149). Just beyond here is Burrell's Wharf.

Burrell's Wharf was the first large-scale iron shipbuilding yard when it opened in 1835. Between 1853 and 1858 Brunel's 680-foot long *Great Eastern* steam ship was built here. In 1888 The Blythe Colour

Works began producing dyes and paints on the site and only closed in 1986. The residential development incorporates some of the old buildings including the Platehouse where steel sheets for the *Great Eastern* and other ships were made.

Until the riverside path at Mackonochie's Wharf and Locke's Wharf is completed, West Ferry Road must be followed to the south of the island. Turn right into Ferry Lane to find The Ferry House pub at the end.

The Ferry House, the oldest pub on the island, once stood alone here at the Greenwich ferry point used by Samuel Pepys in 1665. With the arrival of the railway in 1872 the ferry moved to the east end of the L-shaped street and ceased operation thirty years later when the foot tunnel opened (see below).

Bear left with Ferry Street and turn into the far end of Felsted Wharf to find a riverside path at Livingstone Place affording a superb view of Greenwich. Walk through the middle of the development to return to the street and turn right to walk between a rowing club and Island Gardens Station. Turn right into Island Gardens laid out in 1895 on the spot where Canaletto viewed Greeenwich for his famous painting. Island Gardens Café is open most days.

The walk goes under the river by way of the tunnel reached in the corner of the park. The tunnel, which is at times 60 ft below the surface, emerges by the *Cutty Sark* on the Greenwich bank.

Cutty Sark was launched at Dumbarton in 1869 and has been preserved in this dry dock since 1957 after bringing tea from China and wool from Australia. Open daily; admission £1.40, concessions 40p.

Walk upstream to pass the permanently moored Book Boat. The path leads inland into Horseferry Place, the southern landing of the Greenwich Ferry (see above). Turn right into Thames Street and left into Norway Street to reach the main road. Now turn right to cross Deptford Creek.

Deptford Creek is the mouth of the River Ravensbourne which rises in Farnborough, Kent. The road bridge can be opened for shipping and the upstream railway track, on the London Bridge-Greenwich line, can be lifted in three minutes. Before 1963 the railway operation took an hour.

On the far side of the creek leave the main road by turning down Stowage (right) which leads along the back of Greenwich Power Station to St Nicholas' church at Deptford Green.

Deptford Old Church is, naturally, dedicated to St Nicholas. The tower dates from around 1500 although the top was restored this century. The church is noted for the skulls on the gateposts. Deptford's main church is now St Paul's in the High Street, designed around 1712 by Thomas Archer and described as one of London's finest parish churches.

Go ahead into McMillan Street to briefly join Creek Road. At the crossroads at the end of Deptford High Street turn right down into Watergate Street. Unless visiting Deptford ferry steps ahead, turn left into Prince Street to pass a dock entrance.

Convoys Wharf is a working dock and successor to the Royal Navy Yard founded here by Henry VIII in 1513. Elizabeth I dined on board the *Golden Hind* here. Nearby Czar Street (see below) recalls the long stay of Peter the Great at Sayes Court (see below) in 1698 to study shipbuilding.

Continue along Prince Street to pass Czar Street and at the main road go right into Grove Street to pass the Sayes Court site. After the road bends go right into Leeway and near the end turn left into Pepys Park. Follow the path to walk through the Pepys Estate to the riverside at Deptford Strand where there is a view downstream to Greenwich.

Deptford Strand runs across the front of the Victualling Yard where provisions and clothing for the Royal Navy were stored. The buildings date from the 1780s and remained in use until 1961. Two rum warehouses face the river and in Grove Street at the back there is an impressive gateway leading to a colonnade which housed the Porter and Clerk of the Cheque. Earlier the yard was under the control of Samuel Pepys who stored some of his possessions here during the Great Fire of London.

The promenade continues across Deptford Wharf to St George's Wharf where a boundary stone set in a freestanding wall marks the division between Deptford and Rotherhithe. Keep by the river to go over South Dock's lock gates and along the riverside behind a new development to cross the Greenland Dock entrance footbridge.

Greenland Dock Entrance.

Greenland Dock, named after its whaling trade connections, dates from 1700 and was enlarged in 1904. Surrey Docks Farm (see below) was on the south side of the entrance for ten years soon after the docks closed in 1970.

Keep to the river and soon the riverside path turns inland up an alley known as Randall's Rest. Go right (before The Ship & Whale pub) to follow Odessa Street. Go left with the road and then right into the beginning of Rotherhithe Street which soon bears right towards the river and farm.

Surrey Docks Farm was started on the south side of Greenland Dock entrance (see above) in 1975 and moved here to South Wharf in 1986. The farm is run on organic lines and goats' milk, eggs, cheese and honey can be purchased. Trinity Wharf next door is a business centre which includes a café open to the public on weekdays.

For the next 1¼ miles there are so far few riverside paths although plenty of river glimpses. Stay in Rotherhithe Street to walk upstream. Beyond Trinity Wharf there is the former Durand's Wharf timber yard which has become a park with a riverside path. Logs continued to be landed at next door Lawrence Wharf until 1986. Beyond here is Nelson Dock which will soon be reached by a riverside path.

Nelson Dock. The house was built about 1740 and at first stood flanked by timber yards facing open fields. This was a shipbuilding yard and the dry dock remains.

Just beyond The Blacksmith's Arms (right) is Canada Wharf which has a path running down its north side called Cuckold's Point.

Cuckold's Point is said to date back to King John's reign when the King, caught with a man's wife at their Charlton home, offered him as much land as he could see. This was the furthest point.

Continue along the road where there are now more river views over empty sites towards Wapping. Ignore any turnings at a junction and continue onward to cross the entrance to Surrey Basin. Still stay on the road which passes between new developments to enter Rotherhithe village.

Rotherhithe has had a church for over a thousand years but the present St Mary's was built in 1720 by local shipwrights, hence the ships' masts for pillars inside. Captain Christopher Jones, Master of the *Mayflower* which sailed from here, is commemorated to the left of the sanctuary. John Clarke, who sailed with him and gave his

Free range hens at Surrey Docks Farm.

Parish boundary stone which now marks the Lewisham-Southwark borough border on Surrey Docks waterfront.

name to Clarke's Island, Massachusetts, was a local man. To meet the needs of sailors, The Mayflower pub was once the only one licensed to sell stamps. There are still a few residents who remember when there was a mass exodus to Kent every September for hop picking. Despite the docks' closure the Finnish and Norwegian churches remain in Albion Road on the far side of the Rotherhithe tunnel entrance.

Beyond the Knott Garden (right) opened in 1981 and The Mayflower keep ahead down the alley at the side of the church. At the end bear right to a new arcaded riverside path which affords an unusual view of Tower Bridge. Stay by the river to pass The Angel pub and follow Bermondsey Wall to Cherry Garden Pier.

Cherry Garden Pier was the landing stage for those visiting the nearby Bermondsey Spa in the late 18th century. The Cherry Garden was itself a noted pleasure garden. It was here that J.M.W. Turner painted '*The Fighting* Témérairé'. Ships sound their hooters here if they want Tower Bridge raised.

After a short distance a detour has to be made round Chambers Wharf by way of Loftie Street, Chambers Street (right) and back to Bermondsey Wall (right). Here the walk passes imperceptibly on to Jacob's Island.

Jacob's Island is bounded by the Thames and St Saviour's Dock on two sides but was once surrounded by water at high tide. Dickens highlighted the appalling conditions here in *Oliver Twist*. Now there are a couple of art galleries and a film studio. New Concordia Wharf was one of the first Docklands developments of the 1980s.

Bermondsey Wall leads into Mill Street by New Concordia Wharf. Walk down to the far end of Mill Street and go right into Jamaica Road for a view up St Saviour's Dock.

St Saviour's Dock was first formed by the mouth of the River Neckinger. Bermondsey Abbey maintained a tide mill here.

Return to the river by way of Shad Thames (right) where there is a view down Queen Elizabeth Street (left) to a dray horse statue which recalls the Courage stables on the site until 1987.

Opposite the Design Museum (left) a passage leads back to the riverside at St Saviour's Dock entrance. New Concordia Wharf is on the far bank. Follow the path round to the front or Butler's Wharf.

Butler's Wharf was completed in 1873 and much of the traffic here was foodstuffs. The last ships — East German — called here in 1972. The next door Anchor Brewery dates from at least 1787 when John Courage from Aberdeen bought an existing brewhouse on the site. Sacks of malt were landed from barges. Courage's ceased brewing here in 1981 although bottling continued for a few more years. The stabling of drays nearby (see above) was in keeping with the tradition as indicated by Horselydown Lane.

The path returns to Shad Thames by way of the narrow Maggie Blake's Cause, named after a campaigner for river access. Turn right for Tower Bridge where steps lead up to the road.

Walk 17

Purfleet & Grays

———— 5 miles ————

OS Landranger 177, Pathfinder 1176 and 1177

This is not a beautiful walk but the little-used path gives a last chance to see the industrial working Thames where oil, paper and other cargo land at the numerous jetties. Already there are signs of change as wharves begin to close leaving once fine wooden piers to rot. Here gulls rise in surprise at being disturbed by a stranger and across the river are views of Kent. The walk starts at Purfleet Station but a return should be booked to Grays.

> **Purfleet** stands above the eastern side of the confluence of the Mar Dyke and Thames overlooking Aveley Marshes to the west and the mouth of the River Darent on the far side of the main river. Purfleet was the site of the Government Powder Magazine which has now been converted into modern housing. The baker's was established in 1788 and the early 19th-century colonnaded pub, The Royal, stands by the disused ferry which ran to Longreach on the edge of the Dartford Marshes for over 500 years until this century. The church was built in 1920 with materials from the late 18th-century Purfleet House, home of brewer Samuel Whitbread.

The walk starts by the Purfleet Station signal box. Walk down the path in front of Railway Cottages and bear left to cross a metalled drive. The track meets a gateway by steps (right). Do not go up the steps but round the gates to continue. Keep to the right of the widening space and take a narrow footpath which veers up the bank to a long enclosed path.

Follow this narrow path by the works (right) for ¼ mile to reach a viewpoint (with a surprise seat) by the river. This gives a first chance to see the now wide river and the view over to Littlebrook Power Station on the Dartford Salt Marshes. Beyond here the path is below but still inside the flood defence in front of the Esso refinery with another river view at the first of many jetties. Beyond here there is an alternative outer path although it tends to be overgrown. Where the upper and lower paths join there is another jetty and then a level crossing

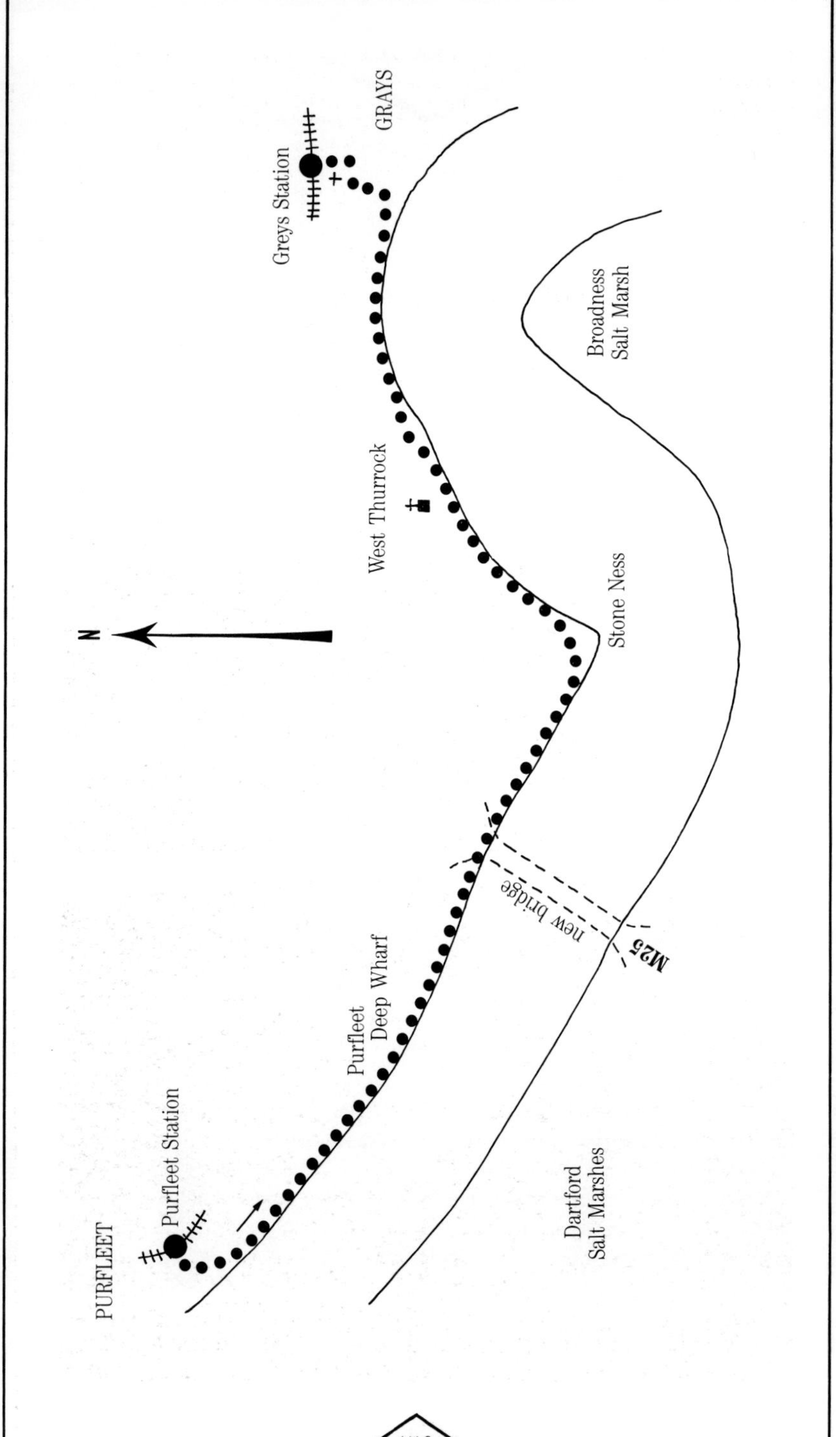

GRAYS

Greys Station

West Thurrock

Broadness
Salt Marsh

Stone Ness

N

Purfleet
Deep Wharf

new bridge

M25

Purfleet Station

PURFLEET

Dartford
Salt Marshes

Right *The remains of Purfleet's 18th century powder magazine.*

Below *Botany cottages at Purfleet.*

A successor to the original Armada Beacon at Purfleet.

where lines run out along a still working wooden pier.

This is Purfleet Deep Wharf and after the level crossing the way affords a view of huge rolls of newsprint stacked like toilet rolls. Again there is a lower shelf alternative path. Extreme care should be taken where the footpath passes through the covered approach to the Roll-on-Roll-off landing stage.

Soon steps take the way over redundant pipes and, later on, under a concrete pier. The path then zig-zags to go outside the flood defences and under the first of two wooden piers. After the second pier, the path rises and falls on a concrete ramp just before passing over the Dartford Tunnel. Here work is in progress on

Purfleet Deep Water Dock.

the new high-level Dartford Bridge to assist the flow of traffic on the M25.

Beyond the new Dartford Bridge site the path passes over an old level crossing where the rails run on to an abandoned pier. At this point there is another choice of parallel paths on either side of the massive concrete wall which gently bends to the right towards the West Thurrock oil terminal pier. Just beyond here it is possible to climb over the wall by ladder for a river view. After 250 yards the wall bears sharply right and left. Here the inner path crosses by ramps to the outside. Across the river, beyond the L-shaped jetty, can be seen Stone in Kent with its church.

The riverside path runs round an inlet. At the next ramp one can go behind the wall for a higher view of the red beacon on Stone Ness headland which soon comes level with the path.

> **Stone Ness.** There is a direct view across to the church at Greenhithe which was linked to this point by a ferry for at least 500 years until the late 19th century. A little to the east of Greenhithe on the green hill is Ingress Abbey built in the 1830s with stone from Old London Bridge. Further west still is the Empire Paper Mills jetty. East on the Essex bank is a view of Grays church below four tower blocks which are further downstream at Tilbury. Immediately inland here at Stone Ness are the West Thurrock Marshes.

The river bends north-east and the path passes Thurrock Power Station. To pass beyond the jetty (where the gates are normally locked) go outside the wall and underneath. Take the next ramp up to the top of the wall to see the isolated West

Tunnel Jetty near the Dartford Tunnel.

West Thurrock Church.

Thurrock church dwarfed by a new warehouse and the Proctor & Gamble soap factory. A path leads inland to the church.

St Clement, West Thurrock. The north aisle windows indicate that the church dates from the 12th century. The 15th-century tower replaced the original circular tower whose exposed base with its recycled Roman tiles can be seen outside the west end. The river used to flow closer to the churchyard at high tide and there was a ferry from here to the inlet at Broadness which is said to have been well used by pilgrims to Canterbury. The West Thurrock houses are now some way from the church which has been declared redundant and placed in the care of its neighbour Proctor & Gamble. Most of the furnishings have gone although the early 17th-century figures of Sir Christopher and Lady Helford still recline in the north transept.

Return to the river to continue downstream. The path runs below the wall at Proctor's. At the far end there is a pier where steps take the path on an inland detour. Follow the enclosed way — there is often a strong smell of soap — to the entrance of Fitzpatrick Asphalt.

Go directly ahead past Fitzpatrick Asphalt (right) and through a very narrow green gate. Here very great care must be taken as the path is not waymarked and infilling has changed the riverline shown on maps. Keep forward (there may be piles of aggregates to climb over) towards the former redundant Blue Circle cement works. Before reaching the buildings turn right on to a slightly overgrown concrete path running directly towards rising steps. (There is a gantry also running in that direction.)

The steps lead to the riverside path outside the flood defence wall. Follow the

Above West
Thurrock.

Right The industrial
riverside at Purfleet.

path round three bends to go under a wooden pier (still in use). Steps take the path up to a concrete road.

Continue walking downstream and ahead where the concrete surface swings inland. Steps carry the path over pipes at a jetty before the way runs below the wall. Ahead is Grays church whilst Tilbury Docks can be seen across the vast expanse of water created by the riverbend round Kent's Broadness Salt Marsh. The path runs through a disused wharf. On coming level with an inlet climb the steps to cross the wall and pass The Wharf pub. Its once-magnificent view from the ground floor is now blocked by the flood defence as is the little wharf where customers could moor their boats.

Continue ahead inside the wall. The path soon leaves the river to run by a new estate built on the docks. On reaching Argent Street turn left up West Street towards the church. The road bends right to a junction by The Rising Sun. Turn left past the pub and the church (left). Grays Station is ahead by the level crossing.

Grays church is mainly a Victorian building of 1846 but has traces of the 12th-century building and 13th-century work. The village was a crossing point to Swanscombe from at least 1200 to the 1600s. The arrival of the railway has divided the old Grays from the new which has spread north and east to merge with Little Thurrock.

TILBURY

───── 6½ miles ─────

OS Landranger 177, Pathfinder 1177

At Tilbury the river feels more like the sea and Gravesend opposite looks like a seaside town. Shipping which would once have been seen in London is still drawn here by Tilbury Docks. The occasional vessel with 'Ford' emblazoned on the side reminds us of the proximity of Dagenham. The Kent bank is explored on Walk 19. This Essex shoreline is one of great contrasts with plenty of wildlife and very good views on clear days. It is not unusual of course for the far bank to be lost in mist. A picnic is advised as the only refreshment is at East Tilbury's pub.

The walk starts at Tilbury Riverside Station but a return should be booked to East Tilbury. Tilbury Riverside is not open on Sundays.

Tilbury novelist Daniel Defoe was a tile works manager here at the end of the 18th century. The docks opened in 1886. On the corner of Calcutta and Docks Roads is a fading wall painting, sponsored by *The Daily Herald*, indicating the once strong Labour and trade union activity in the town. Tilbury Riverside Station with its cupolas was built in the late 1920s to a design by Sir Edwin Cooper. BR notices in Russian are a reminder that Russian ships still call here. BR runs the foot ferry to Gravesend (see page 171) having inherited the service from the London, Tilbury and Southern Railway Company. However the ferry has operated since Tudor times when Tilbury Fort was built. In 1623 one of the passengers was the future Charles I travelling in disguise to Spain to check on the suitability of the Infanta as a bride. Suspicion was aroused when his companion, the Duke of Buckingham, paid the fare with a gold coin. The ferry once carried cattle and, until 1962, cars.

On leaving the platform turn left out of Tilbury Riverside Station and through the flood defences to the approach road. Follow the flood wall on the right — steps lead to the outside. The low-lying Tilbury Fort can be seen below the

A British Rail notice in Russian at Tilbury Riverside Station (Marion Marples).

towering Tilbury Power Station. At The Worlds End pub (dating from 1694 and built for the ferrymen) the path moves inside the wall but with a high path. Walk round to come level with the Fort gatehouse.

The World's End pub at Tilbury.

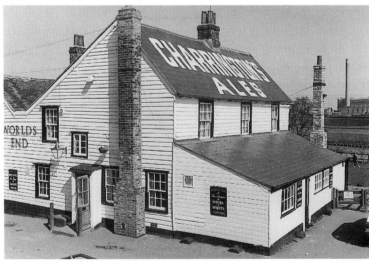

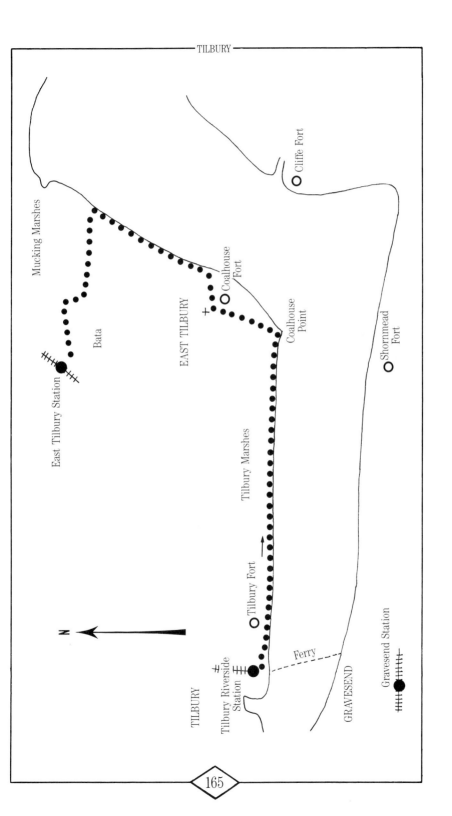

Left *The gatehouse to Tilbury Fort.*

Below right
Coalhouse Point.

Tilbury Fort. Henry VIII built the first here as a defence and it was this small building that existed when Elizabeth I came here in 1588 to encourage the 17,000 troops who were to stop the Spanish Armada from coming up the Thames. It was on this occasion that the Queen made her famous speech, declaring, 'I know I have the body of a weak and feeble woman but I have the heart and stomach of a King, a King of England too!' The present fort with its impressive gateway was completed in 1683 as the result of a Dutch raid in 1667. However in 1689 the Dutch King, William III, succeeded to the English throne. Open daily; admission £1.10 with concessions for children and OAPs.

Continue on the promenade past the fort to where there is a good view of the eastern moat and (sometimes) its swans. The surface becomes rough and at the side of Tilbury Power Station the path continues in front of the wall. Take the steps down to the concrete path in the inlet and follow the way round the corner to continue upstream.

On reaching a substantial jetty climb the steps to go over the wall and follow a short path leading to covered steps which cross the jetty approach. On the far side there is a railing to climb over at the bottom of the flight of steps. Take more steps over the river wall. Follow the wall until it joins natural shoreline. This has the nature of a low seaside cliff — a feeling enhanced by the rise and fall of the tide on the beach. Go through the gap in the fence to find the outline of a lost barge in the beach which is often littered with fragments of washed-up china. Inland, sometimes, are grazing horses and sheep. At first the path is hardly defined but after about ¼ mile there is a clear path running parallel to the river.

At a stream, which divides the West and East Tilbury Marshes and now completes its journey to the Thames by pipe, follow the wall to a stile. Walk across a concrete area by an abandoned jetty. The path runs directly ahead by the water with East Tilbury Marshes, now raised from dumping, behind a wire fence where tomatoes can be seen growing.

After just over ¼ mile the ground on the left falls away to its original level to reveal farmland and East Tilbury's church and fort in the trees. The path goes ahead on an embankment towards the beacon on Coalhouse Point.

Coalhouse Point was the unloading point for coal from the north well into this century. It is also the site of a fort built by Henry VIII at the same time as the first Tilbury Fort. The beacon is a low-level radar station erected in 1939.

On coming level with Coalhouse Point (where there is a rare footpath sign) do not continue ahead but take the path running inland. The way is a former railway track which linked Coalhouse Point to Coalhouse Fort.

Coalhouse Fort was built under the supervision of General Gordon between 1866 and 1871 as the main defence of London against the French. Cliffe and Shornmead Forts on the Kent side (see page 175) would have created a triangle of fire. The fire beacon was erected in 1988 for the Armada anniversary although in 1588 there was probably no such beacon here — the nearest being in Kent at High

Coalhouse Fort.

Hastow and Dartford. The Fort now houses the Thameside Aviation Museum and a collection of military vehicles. Open on the last Sunday afternoon of the month; admission 75p.

Behind the Fort is an incongruous 'Superloo' and the beginning of East Tilbury village.

Ancient ferry road at East Tilbury.

East Tilbury is largely a model village laid out by Bata Shoes.

East Tilbury's new housing is hidden behind the escarpment. The church, next to the fort, has a blocked Norman window, and a blocked arch at the west end suggests that there was a 13th-century tower which must have been a landmark for shipping. It still has an Elizabethan pulpit. The church is thought to have been damaged by the Dutch when they attacked Tilbury (see page 166). Before the fort was built the tidal water may have come a little nearer the church and until the 16th century the road led to the ferry to Higham (see page 175). The Romans crossed here and the long village street, now called Princess Margaret Road, is probably prehistoric. The Ship pub is 300 yards up the road and East Tilbury Station is 1½ miles beyond near the Bata shoe factory model village.

The walk continues downstream. Take the metalled path running between the church and the fort and after a short distance bear left over the grass to the flood defence. (The path can also be joined from a gate in the churchyard.)

A good concrete path runs outside the river defence wall. The way soon turns north round a bay which is slowly being infilled. Across the river can be seen the jetty at Cliffe Fort and a lonely coastguard house on Cliffe Marshes. Inland beyond the farmland is the Bata shoe factory, a model establishment begun in 1931 and partly resembling its factory in Czechoslovakia.

The river widens considerably as it begins to turn east on its final bend before the North Sea. Ahead are the oil refineries at Shellhaven. On coming level with Lower Hope Point on the Kent bank, the new river defence ends. Here the footpath usually runs ahead to turn inland at Mucking Marshes but for the present the land is being covered with London's rubbish brought here by barge. The long term diversion means that the path turns inland where the flood

Rotting jetty near Mucking Marshes.

defence ends. Follow the track by the wire fence (right). Eventually the winding path and fence turn sharply right to a cross track by gates. Here, where there should be a footpath sign, turn left on to the old path which soon runs along the side of a housing estate. After just over ¼ mile the path reaches double gates by Princess Margaret Road. Turn right for the station which is a few yards away by a still manned level crossing.

GRAVESEND & CLIFFE

——— 15 miles ———

OS Landranger 177 and 178, Pathfinder 1177

This is a long walk on one of the loneliest downstream reaches of the river with two little-known abandoned forts lying far out on the marshes away from the villages from which they take their names. On a clear day interest is heightened if the opposite shore has already been explored on Walk 18. The entire route is definitely an all-day walk which may need a picnic as there is no refreshment until remote Cliffe which, surprisingly, manages to maintain three pubs and several shops. In spite of new housing Cliffe remains an instantly recognizable Kent village and Higham has changed little since Charles Dickens visited. The outward route as far as Cliffe follows the Saxon Shore Way (see page 180).

The walk starts at Gravesend Station. Maidstone & District Buses run routes 317 and 318 to Cliffe from Gravesend (Mondays to Saturdays) so the walk can be split into two outings. Also, the walk can be shortened by three miles by catching a train at Higham.

Gravesend is the first port of importance on the Thames and here ships bound for London Docks would take on a pilot. The French sailed up and attacked in 1380 and the Dutch attack in 1667 led to new fortifications on both sides of the river (see pages 167 and 175). The town looks its best from Tilbury, opposite, for a great fire in 1727 destroyed much of the centre including St George's church which was rebuilt in 1732. Since then the position of Princess Pocahontas' coffin under the chancel has been uncertain. She was the first Red Indian princess to visit England and died here on board ship at the end of her visit in 1617. The churchyard is now the Princess Pocahontas Gardens and has a replica of her statue in Jamestown.

On leaving Gravesend Station (downside) turn right and go left just past the shopping centre into Stone Street. At the main road continue down Princes Street at the side of the Army & Navy Store to pass the church (left). Cross the

Tilbury ferry preparing to leave for Gravesend.

road ahead to go down Talbot Place at the side of The New Falcon pub for a first view of the river at the Tilbury Ferry pier. Across the river is Tilbury Riverside station and the low-lying Tilbury Fort. Between the two can be seen The Worlds End pub (see page 164).

To continue the walk return to the main road and turn left to go downstream and pass the Town Pier flanked by The Pier Hotel and The Three Daws, Kent's

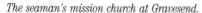

The seaman's mission church at Gravesend.

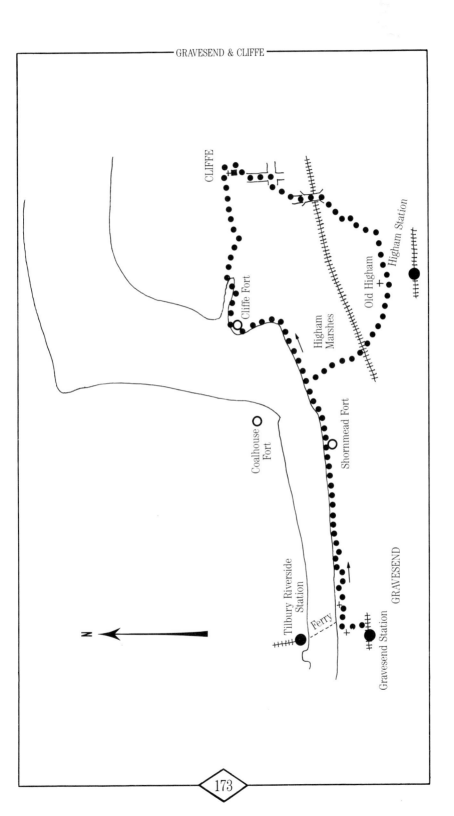

oldest pub dating from at least the Tudor period. Where the main road bears right walk down a slope and steps into Royal Pier Road. Sticking out into the river is the former St Andrew's church, opened in 1871 as a mission to seamen and now an arts centre.

A little further ahead is The Clarendon Royal Hotel which began as accommodation for the Duke of York, the future James II. Across the road is the remains of a Tudor blackhouse built as part of the defences to back up the other forts including Tilbury.

The road rises to pass the Royal Terrace Pier and turn inland. At the crossroads go left down The Terrace and left again at the bottom of the street to pass the back of the Milton Chantry (left). The 14th-century chapel, now incorporated into a fort by General Gordon, looks more recent and secular from the road. Go through the gateway ahead and bear right with the wide path to reach Gordon Promenade.

At the far end by the sailing club go over a swing bridge at the harbour entrance to follow a partly cobbled way along the back of working wharves. Beware of lorries crossing the path at the end where the way turns right. An enclosed passage leads into Wharf Road by a ship repair yard (left). Follow the road to a junction and turn left. A notice points to 'Care Auto Repair'.

The road passes two houses and bears right. Walk behind the white building ahead to follow the flood defence wall. Beware of lorries crossing the path to and from Denton Wharf. After a second lorry crossing point the path passes in front of The Ship & Lobster — the last refreshment point before Cliffe. Continue up a few steps and on reaching a Saxon Shore stone go over the flood defence wall which turns inland. From now on the flood defence is a long grass bank with the grass kept short by grazing horses and ponies as well as winter wind.

Looking across the river from Gravesend to Tilbury Docks.

Higham Marshes in Kent with Coalhouse Fort in Essex in the distance.

The path runs under a gantry and past a pier. Soon the way is alongside the Eastcourt marshes used as an Army shooting range. Across the usually busy river are the East Tilbury Marshes. At one point it is necessary to squeeze past the end of a fence which runs up to the shore. Here the high bank is replaced by dumped stones but, just before reaching Shornmead Fort, the path rises again on to a high bank.

Shornmead Fort lies low on the edge of Shorne Marshes which are still used for military training although the fort is abandoned. (See Coalhouse Fort, page 167).

Continue ahead with the dual bank which merges at a bend. Inland can be seen Higham church (reached on the return; see page 177) whilst the path runs towards the beacon. The fence is crossed by means of a stile on the innerside of the bank. After ¼ mile the footpath from Higham can be seen joining at a gate below (right). Outside the bank is the outline of a creek where the ferry from Coalhouse Point once landed (see page 167).

The path continues along the bottom of Higham Marshes on one side of a right-angled bay. At the corner, where there is a concrete base, bear left with the water. Soon there is a group of wartime concrete tank traps and a fence to climb through. Then the path runs between both the river and a flooded pit (right) for just over ½ mile to reach the looming Cliffe Fort opposite Coalhouse Fort on the Essex bank (see page 167).

Walk round the outside of the fort and past the pier. Steps lead across the end of a slipway. Walk forward to a jetty entrance and (watching for lorries) go inland on the approach road for a few yards before turning left under the high conveyor to pass the side of a hut. Here a path runs ahead on a high bank and curves inland with the Cliffe Creek entrance. Cliffe church can be seen on the high chalk cliff beyond the marshes.

Continue up the creek and soon the path runs away from the water. Where the path emerges at the start of a long straight track by a field turn left to return to the bankside. (The straight path is not a short cut.) Just before the end of the creek the path turns across the water to the far bank. An arrow on a low concrete wall now indicates the direction to be taken.

Go half left over the wall and wide track below to walk up a narrower path opposite. Bear right at the next junction (by a broken Saxon Shore stone). Now the track runs between low trees with occasional views over flooded pits towards Cliffe. At a T-junction below a low cliff turn left along a wider track. The cliff soon becomes higher and after the way turns north, go right at a junction. High on the cliff is a lonely radar station. After ¼ mile Cliffe church comes into view and the path turns up into the village. Upstream across the marsh is a view of Shellhaven on the Essex shore.

Cliffe was some way from the river even in Roman times although the water could cover the marshland at the bottom of the main street which retains its Kentish weatherboarded buildings. The impressive church is 13th and 14th century with the usual Victorian restoration. It owes its size to the fact that the manor belonged to Canterbury — two rectors went on to become archbishops at Canterbury and York. Writer Fanny Burney's brother was the incumbent in the late 18th century.

Continue up the main street and round the double bend by The Six Bells. Follow the straight road south for ½ mile to a crossroads. On the way there are views eastwards to Cooling church.

Kentish weatherboarded buildings at Cliffe.

Go right at the crossroads and where the houses on the left end go left. A narrow path leads past a line of gardens (left). At the end go over a stile into an orchard and follow a path ahead which after a double bend runs south. Do not go through a gate at the top end but turn right to a stile in the south-west corner. Cross the stile and turn left over a road entrance to walk up the road past Buckland Farm. Cross the bridge (over the single track railway to the Isle of Grain oil refinery) and go over a wooden stile by a gate on the right.

The way is now half left down the hill across the field just touching the circular object in the middle. Unfortunately this path is regularly ploughed and the farmer prefers walkers to go round the edge. Just before the pylon cross a footbridge over a stream. Go ahead by the thin copse (left) to a little used stile by a wooden bridge.

Over the bridge the way is now half right up the hill and through the long line of trees. However this route is often under cultivation and instead local walkers turn right and then go left by a new hedge to reach the end of the line of trees near Oakleigh Farm (right). Walk along the line of trees to find a path running to the right downhill to a metalled driveway near a house (right).

Go right along the metalled path to pass the house (right) and where the way divides go left on to a rough path. Soon the way passes a pond (right) by a turning to the farm buildings. Keep ahead on the path but when the track turns sharply right still continue ahead to reach Higham's Church Street.

Church Street, Higham, is 'Old' Higham. The church, with its short shingled spire which serves as a landmark to shipping, stands on the edge of the marshes. The building dates from Saxon times and

Higham Church.

is unusual in having an old and new chancel — the former retains its rood screen. This church, although usually open, is now redundant with services held at the Victorian St John's church 1¾ miles to the south. But this old village retains its thatched weatherboarded Old Rectory and Clerk's Cottage. Abbey Farm to the east of the church is on the site of a nunnery opened in 1148 with sixteen sisters and closed in 1521 when there were just four. The Sun Inn is one of the least spoilt and commercialized in Kent. Dickens, who lived at the 'new' Higham inland, is said to have used local features in *Great Expectations*.

Higham Station, which has two trains an hour daily, is one mile to the south at Lower Higham. Trains to London emerge from a long tunnel designed to carry a canal cut from the River Medway to the Thames. The engineer was William Tierney Clark who was responsible for the Thames bridges at Marlow and Hammersmith (see pages 84 and 133).

At the road junction go ahead by the grass triangle to pass the Old Vicarage (right) and the Clerk's Cottage. Beyond the (easily missed) pub, the road passes a farmyard (often guarded by geese) and becomes a grass track. After ¼ mile the path meets the single-track railway line. Do not go up the bank to the gate but through the hidden tunnel to an iron gate on the far side.

Ahead can be seen the red beacon near Shornmead Fort. Walk towards it for 200 yards to join a firmer path which swings in from the left and at first appears to be heading for a point well to the right of the beacon. On the left of the track

Cliffe Fort.

is a water-filled ditch. Soon the path draws level with a barrow (right) rising out of Higham Marshes. At a bend in this old ferry path there is an iron gate (usually open). Cliffe Fort becomes more visible half right and the Coalhouse Point radar beacon can be seen peeping over the high riverside bank. On approaching the river go over a stile by a gate and climb up on to the riverside path.

Turn left to walk upstream over the outward route. Gravesend can be reached in about an hour.

HERNE BAY & ISLE OF THANET

———— 12 miles ————

OS Landranger 179, Pathfinder 1195 and 1196

Just as some question the authencity of the official Thames source and suggest nearby streams may have a better claim, so opinions differ over where the estuary ends. Now that the Isle of Thanet is joined to the mainland one can count Margate as a strong candidate for the climax — or start — of a full Thames walk. Certainly the north Kent resorts were considered part of the Thames in the 19th century when most visits were made by ship down the river. This walk, as far as Reculver, largely follows the Saxon Shore Way which traces the old shoreline from Gravesend round to Rye. The natural halfway point on this walk is Reculver where there is a pub and snack bar and in summer a bus service to Herne Bay.

The walk starts at Herne Bay Station but a return should be booked to Margate. There are also handy stations at Birchington and Westgate.

> **Herne Bay**, north of the village of Herne, was the first sheltered port for coal ships making for London from the north. One route to the continent was by ship from London to here and then stagecoach to Dover. The passenger traffic from London was badly hit by the arrival of the railway in the mid 19th century which led to the town's growth. The oldest part is still to be found around The Ship Inn. The main streets were laid out on a grid system in 1833, a year after the almost mile-long pier opened. The remains of the pier, finally demolished in 1979 after storm damage, can be seen ¾ mile off Herne Bay.

On leaving Herne Bay Station turn right to follow Station Road to the seafront. Turn right along the road and beyond the Tourist Information Office go over the sea wall to walk along the promenade behind the Clock Tower — built in 1837 to mark Queen Victoria's accession. Just beyond The Ship, the traffic swings inland and a more modest promenade continues past an attractive terrace and the King's Hall (where there is a café).

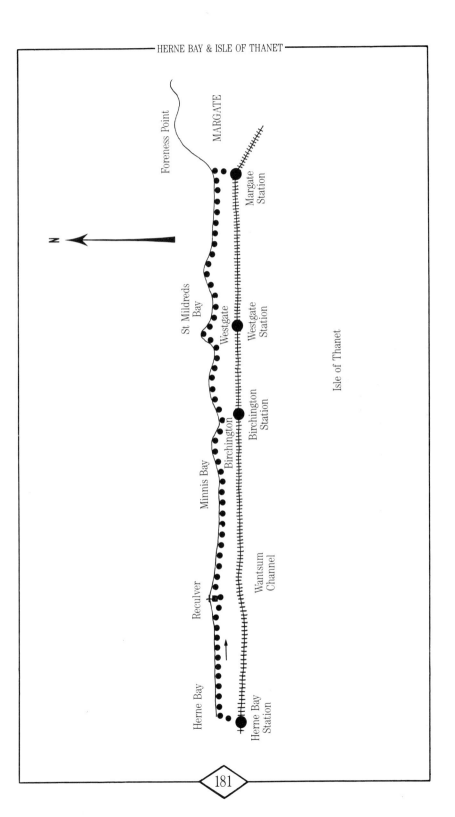

Wooden cliff steps at the end of Herne Bay.

The low promenade continues ahead past the sailing club and between the shingle beach and sloping grass cliffs, known as The Downs, for 1½ miles. Ahead can be seen the twin towers of Reculver which before the end of the promenade disappear behind the cliff ahead. On top of the nearby cliff is an 'Armada' beacon on roughly the correct 1588 site.

At the end of Beltinge Cliff (right) the Saxon Shore Way is waymarked up a steep concrete path; keep forward past this point to the very end of the concrete

The abbey ruins at Reculver seen from the footpath.

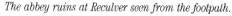

promenade. Here, at the entrance to a deep ravine, climb the wooden steps to the top of the now sheer cliff. Follow the concrete path below the houses to Bishopstone Manor at the end. Continue along the ledge parallel with the cliff edge (left). Inland is a view of Hillborough church which succeeded Reculver's abbey church in the last century.

The path runs past the former coastguard lookout where there is a view down on to Reculver and ahead across the old sea channel to the Isle of Thanet. At this point one can look back to Herne Bay's stranded pier and ahead to Margate. Notices advising one to keep away from the cliff edge should be taken seriously. Continue down the hill to find steps (left) at the bottom leading on to a short promenade. The King Ethelbert is at the end.

Reculver. The sea was a mile away when the Romans built a fort here to guard the channel between the mainland and the Isle of Thanet to the east. St Augustine founded St Mary's Abbey on land given by King Ethelbert but Danish raids probably caused the monks to retreat to the Canterbury mother house just before the Conquest and the church was given to the parish. By the Tudor period the building was still ¾ mile from the sea but by 1809 the water was so close that the church was, with reluctance, partly dismantled and moved south to Hillborough. However the 12th-century twin towers which had long been a landmark for shipping were left in the care of Trinity House.

Walk up the metalled path at the side of the abbey church and continue to go down the slope to the edge of the old mainland. The Saxon Shore Path turns

Looking west from the old seabed towards Reculver.

Reculver's landmark towers.

right with the old coast whilst the walk goes to the left towards the sea beyond a gateway by a thatched hut. A sea wall path runs for 2¾ miles to the Isle of Thanet across the Wantsum Channel.

Wantsum Channel was once part of the North Sea with Reculver as the north-eastern tip of Kent. The crossing to the Isle of Thanet would normally have been made between Upstreet, where a Roman road ran down to the water, and Sarre. But by the 15th-century this channel was so silted up that the Sarre ferry was discontinued in favour of a bridge. Now the water is made up of the tiny River Wantsum and, to the south, the River Stour with most of the old seabed now under cultivation. The sea last broke through the wall in 1953. Thanet is where St Augustine landed from Rome in 597 and the Spanish Armada intended landing its troops at Westgate and Margate in 1588. J.M.W. Turner claimed that 'the loveliest sunsets in Europe are over the Isle of Thanet'.

On the way across, St Nicholas Wade church on Thanet can be seen half right and below the path for a time is the River Wantsum. At the far end of the causeway the path runs on to the grass high ground known as Plumpudding Island on the tip of Thanet. Follow the low cliff round Minnis Bay on the outskirts of Birchington.

Beyond the Minnis Bar and Café go down on to the promenade which continues below the chalk cliffs at the far end of the bay. (If there is a high stormy sea walkers should take the road above the cliff.) The concrete promenade is free of commercialization usually associated with the seaside for this is protection for the chalk cliffs and the beach below is rocky with a partly exposed chalk floor. Low tide attracts oyster-catchers, gulls and other sea birds. The splendid shelf footpath runs round Grenham Bay before turning a corner to the Birchington slipway.

Birchington-on-Sea was developed as a seaside resort in the late 1860s just in advance of Westgate to the east. The land was owned by architect J.P. Seddon who laid out the road system north of the railway. His four remaining substantial Indian-style dwellings known as the Tower Bungalows from their decoration can be seen in Spencer Road just above the cliff. In a now demolished one poet and painter Dante Gabriel Rossetti spent the last month of his life. He is buried outside the church porch in a grave marked by a Celtic cross designed by Ford Madox Brown. Inside the church, which dates from Norman times, is a memorial window based on a drawing by Rossetti. More recently Dennis Wheatley set part of his *Contraband* novel in Birchington and its Quex Park.

The path inland at the slipway leads directly to Birchington Station. Seddon's bungalows are at the end of the first turning left where there are paths back to the seafront.

Detail of one of the houses at Birchington designed by J.P. Seddon.

The main walk continues below the cliff which has several blocked tunnels running inland as well as three remaining access points. The promenade runs round a sharp corner in to Epple Bay where steps lead up to the top of the cliff. Turn left along the cliff top road which runs for ¾ mile to Westgate Bay.

Westgate-on-Sea was developed as a seaside resort in the 1870s and St Saviour's church followed in the early 1880s.

To reach Westgate Station turn right at Domneva Road and left into Cuthbert Road which leads to Station Road.

To continue the walk into Margate one can follow a continuous new promenade from Westgate Bay but the best views are from the clifftop. At the far side of the bay leave the pavement for a cliff path which rises to run over grass above Ledge Point where there is a last view back to Reculver. Continue forward past a pavilion (left) to follow a high path round St Mildred's Bay.

At Pav's Tea Garden (founded in 1950 and noted for its good value trays of tea) briefly join the promenade and follow the way ahead past the headland (left) to a metalled path running along the grass top cliff at Westbrook Bay. Margate and its funfair wheel can be seen ahead. Where the path joins the nearby road by The Ramblers Hotel (right) take the ramp down on to the promenade to walk below the Royal Sea Bathing Hospital. (If there is a high stormy sea the road can be followed round to the front of the hospital.)

Pav's Tea Garden at Westgate.

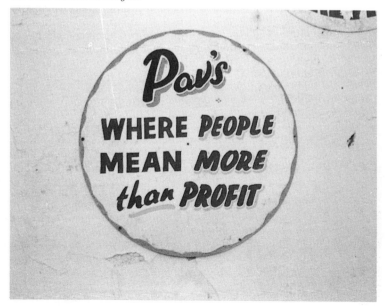

Royal Sea Bathing Hospital, once the General Sea Bathing Infirmary, dates from 1792 although the frontage is an 1820s addition. This was the first hospital to specialize in the treatment of tuberculosis.

The promenade passes the crumbling Royal Crescent to meet the road in Margate. The station is across the road opposite The Sundeck 'pier'.

Margate was a fishing village which, thanks to good shipping links with London, became a successful seaside resort in the 18th century, well in advance of the railway age. At first it was hoys, flat-bottomed sailing ships also used for cargo, which first brought visitors from London on the ten-hour journey. From about 1814 steamers started a service from London Bridge and St Katharine Dock (see page 140). The pier here was finally destroyed in a memorable storm of 1978 which, as at Herne Bay, left its far end marooned. In King Street there is a Tudor timber-framed house and Hawley Street has India House, built in 1767 in imitation of a Calcutta house. The 1786 Theatre Royal, where Bernard Shaw once held a play rehearsal, was completely restored in 1988. Albert Terrace by the clock tower was known as 'Hazardous Terrace' because the sea comes so close to the north end. The little harbour

The archbishop with Margate's Greek community blessing the sea at Epiphany.

was built in 1805 and an early attraction was the mysterious grotto discovered in 1835 and still open during the summer. Margate has a small Greek community which every January holds the traditional Epiphany blessing of the sea ceremony on the beach.

The Thames can be said to finally give way to the North Sea at Foreness Point which is reached by following Fort Hill above the harbour and coastal path round the top of Walpole and Palm Bays. At Foreness there are plenty of kestrels and shorebirds and usually a good view.

SELECT BIBLIOGRAPHY

Astbury, A.K., *Estuary: Land & water in the lower Thames basin* (The Carnforth Press, 1980).

Ebel, Suzanne and Impey, Doreen, *A Guide to London's Riverside* (Constable, 1985).

Eagle, Dorothy and Carnell, Hiliary, *The Oxford Literary Guide* (Oxford University Press, 1981).

Hayward, Graham, *Stanford's River Thames* (Stanford Maritime, 1988).

Jebb, Miles, *A Guide to the Thames Path* (Constable, 1988).

Martin, Nancy, *River Ferries* (Terence Dalton, 1980).

London Dockland Street Atlas & Guide (Nicholas, 1988).

Perrott, David (Editor), *Ordnance Survey Guide To The River Thames* (Nicholson, 1984).

Phillips, Geoffrey, *Thames Crossings* (David & Charles, 1981).

Pritchard, Mari and Carpenter, Humphrey, *A Thames Companion* (Oxford University Press, 1981).

Prockter, Adrian, *A Guide To The River Thames: From Battersea to Woolwich* (London Reference Books, 1983).

Sharp, David, *The Thames Walk* (The Ramblers' Association, 1985).

INDEX

Italics indicate an illustration or photograph.